# Anxious to do Good

## Learning to be an Economist the Hard Way

Alan Peacock

imprint-academic.com

Published in the UK by
Imprint Academic, PO Box 200, Exeter EX5 5YX, UK

Published in the USA by Imprint Academic,
Philosophy Documentation Center
PO Box 7147, Charlottesville, VA 22906-7147, USA

ISBN 9781845401887

A CIP catalogue record for this book is available from the
British Library and US Library of Congress

# Contents

*Dedicated to the Memory of*

*Jo Grimond, Graham Hutton and Frank Paish*

# *Preface*

Alongside professional activities as an economist, I have written two 'quasi-autobiographical' books about particular periods in my life. This is the third one.

Their description by an adjective containing 21 letters requires explanation. The author of the books is depicted as a commentator on events rather than as the central figure in the events themselves. He is not an interesting enough person to accompany the reader on a journey round his skull, and does not want to embarrass those close to him. Self-analysis can encourage presentation of a litany of boring egocentricities, though personal motivation must be part of the story to be told.

Music lovers may recall that Berlioz wrote one of the first romantic concerti for the viola. In 'Harold in Italy' — to the initial disappointment of its sponsor, Paganini — the viola soloist offers a commentary on events in Harold's wanderings, and does not dominate the development of the thematic material. The analogy will not satisfy some readers, any more than Paganini was by 'Harold' — although he changed his mind later. I confess, however, that the analogy is only an approximate guide. Perhaps I should say that the commentary I offer on events has to be accompanied by my reaction to them, if I am to follow my own remit.

That remit has the same pattern as the two previous attempts. Both of them had me accidentally faced with taking part in events which were of public concern. My first attempt shows how my revealed interest in music led me to apply my professional skills in economics to the analysis of the performing arts, to offering commentary on public policy towards the arts, and eventually to membership of the Arts Council of Great Britain and Chair of the Scottish Arts Council.[1] My second concerned a period of my life almost 40 years earlier, but was a totally unexpected occurrence. The now-famous story of the code-cracking activities at Bletchley, known as the *Enigma* breakthrough, became public knowledge nearly 40 years after WW2, it being claimed that these activities shortened that war by two years. What was not known in detail then, not even to those cracking the code, was how the information provided by the enemy of its own activities was used. That side of the story, as it affected Naval operations, is partly told by one who found himself, then only 20, transformed from being an immature university student into a practised hand at puzzling out the meaning of encoded messages while a sea-going intelligence officer. This had to be carried out as quickly as possible if these were to be of potential benefit to convoys facing the icy and tempestuous seas of the Arctic and faced with U boat attacks.[2] While the passing of the years has tested one's memory of events, and available records of them were not always easy to come by, time does improve perspective. It helped me to realise how much one had gained from being a member of a revered tribal society such as the Royal Navy, and also able to examine its influence on one's later attempts to make a living as an analyst of economic behaviour.

This third attempt is more like the second than the first. Chronologically, it is nearer the second but it is less an essay in how one is compelled to face situations that have a profound effect on one's current activities and is more a positive attempt to mould one's own passage through life. This explains the title. Like many whose temporary occupation was on active war service, I was much influenced by a desire to celebrate survival by entering some occupation where I might do some good. One was not quite sure how this was to be done, but in my case, I had embarked on a

---

[1]   See my *Paying the Piper, Culture, Music and Money*, Edinburgh University Press, 1993.

[2]   See my *The Enigmatic Sailor*, Whittles Publishing, 2003.

degree in economics and history before joining the Navy. When demobbed in order to complete my studies, I had already read some of the work of Keynes and Hayek and studied the famous Beveridge Report.

Although unsure of what qualifications would suit the aim of doing good, I was clear on one matter. It would require some form of political action and attachment to a political party. Dundee, where I was brought up, was then represented by a Liberal MP, Dingle Foot, and my parents were staunch Liberals. I seemed to be destined to look for some sort of link with the Liberal Party, and the matter was settled in my mind by the decision of both Keynes and Beveridge to sit as Liberals in the House of Lords.

It is one thing to have aspirations, another to fulfil them, as the first two chapters in this book explain. One must have the training, experience and personality to offer services as an adviser, and there is no guarantee that having the necessary qualities will produce the welcome mat when one taps on the doors of a political party. Half a century ago, even the major political parties had few paid staff, mostly employed in lowly occupations, and they relied on their 'gurus' to give their advice free. A tyro from a small country and 500 miles from London was not going to single-handedly buck the trend, particularly one wishing an attachment to the small residue of Liberal MPs close to the brink of political oblivion. The most one could expect would be to have paid employment which displayed some complementarities with a knowledge of national policy issues. In economics parlance, the opportunity cost of becoming an unpaid adviser was high indeed, given the competition between the time alone devoted to holding down a job, getting relevant experience in advice-giving that would appeal to political clients, not to speak of the loss of hours better spent with a very young family.

I was lucky, for as a junior lecturer in economics, first at my *Alma Mater*, St Andrews, and then at the LSE, I had chosen to specialise on the economics of public policy, particularly social policy, and discovered a ready market for an appraisal of the rationale and the effects of the profound

changes that post-war policies produced on our economic
and social life. By my second year at the LSE, I found myself
invited to be the number-cruncher and statistician of the
Liberal Party Committee on the proposed amalgamation of
Income Tax and Social Security. This launched me on a parallel career to my academic one as a writer, broadcaster, and
lecturer on the welfare state. I 'graduated' from committee
member to informal adviser to Liberal members of Parliament, notably Jo Grimond and membership of the nearest
thing to a Liberal Think Tank, the Unservile State Group.
The pinnacle of my career within this small, if now slowly
growing, coterie of academic economists, economic journalists and politicians, was to address the Liberal Summer
School in 1960, having by then achieved some academic
respectability as Professor of Economic Science at the University of Edinburgh, and about to emigrate south once
again to become the Foundation Professor of Economics at
the new University of York in 1962. I hope that the succeed-
ing chapters (3–8) provide more entertainment than this
bald summary suggests. 'Progress' was rapid but not along
the straight line suggested by an entry in *Who's Who*, being
punctuated with several gaffes and accompanying embar-
rassments.

My 'downfall' is attributable to my attempt, first adum-
brated in the lecture to the Liberal Summer School, to translate liberalist ideas into the design of social policy.[3] This
went far beyond the confines of a liberal approach to the distribution of income and capital, as generally understood, to
cover the distribution of 'human capital' whose contribution to welfare depended on the quality of education, training and research. The issue here went further than the
traditional questions of how far improvement in welfare
required government intervention to the question of the
degree and the form of intervention. There is a vast literature on the philosophy of liberalism covering the relationship between the individual and the state, much of it devoid
of consideration of the institutional framework that liberal-

[3]   Published as *The Welfare Society, Unservile State Papers No 2*, 1961,
      reprinted in revised form, 1966.

ism proposed. The practical point at issue in the 1960s was that of whether the state should have a major role not simply in correcting inequalities in the distribution of individual wealth, but in exercising close control over the way that individuals used their income and capital. In very general terms, one had to consider the balance between state provision of services with a redistributory impact, eg free state education, and state financing of such services that the individual or family could provide for themselves.

So the concentration in the later chapters (8–11) on the then burning issue of educational opportunity during the 1960s is designed to cover the more fundamental question of the ultimate aim of a Liberal policy for the welfare state as well as the provision of educational services in particular.

I severed any formal connection with the Liberal party because their senior politicians of the time, regrettably lead by Nancy Seear—an old friend and colleague, later to become Liberal Party Leader in the House of Lords— rejected my advice. It was not simply a question of the inevitable gap between what is desirable and what is feasible at the particular moment when increasing Liberal political representation depended on other issues, notably our parlous economic position internationally. It was that a belief in the co-incidence of the desirable and feasible as a long-term aim was lacking. The touchstone in the contemporary argument was whether parents should have freedom of choice in education and students should pay for their education being subsidised only to the extent that there was a community interest in their choice of study area. The voucher system was something of a compromise because the financial support it offered was based on the assumption that there was a community interest in education that required compulsory schooling.

Nancy and her supporters claimed that parents did not make wise choices for their children, thereby rejecting the fundamental principle of consumer sovereignty. Moreover, private educational provision was mired by pursuit of objectives by the supplier, that ensured pupils would be exploited as sources of profit and would be brainwashed so as to promote adherence to out-of-date conceptions of class distinctions. In short, there was no way in which a liberal society resting on self-help and concern for others expressed through voluntary action was achievable. The whole argument is set out in some detail in the final chapters, and the only point I wish to make here is to reiterate that the dispute, conducted in the most friendly terms, was more than a scrap about a minor issue concerning welfare state finance. It leaves as unanswered the question: Is Liberal politics the true practical expression of liberal philosophy?

# Acknowledgments

The idea for writing up my close encounters with the Liberal Party arose from several conversations with Trevor Smith (Lord Smith of Clifton), Liberal Democrat spokesman on Northern Ireland matters in the House of Lords. I am particularly glad to have had his support for the project. He turned my steps towards the Joseph Rowntree Reform Trust which led to the award of a grant from their Research Fund. I owe a debt of gratitude to the Trustees of the Trust for this support. It enabled me to perform the leg work and that of others who helped me in tracking down and transcribing documents, everything from unpublished memoirs to newspaper cuttings.

The Liberal Party archives are now held by the Robbins Library of the London School of Economics and Political Science (LSE), whose archivists provided valuable services in identifying relevant material. In particular, they shamed me into recognizing how poor were my records of my own involvement with Liberal Party matters, for I was able to lay my hands on copies of several of my own articles in discontinued Party publications.

It would have deterred those who might find this work of interest if I had backed up every statement with elaborate footnotery. Instead, I have offered a selection of my own publications relating to the subject matter, several of them not previously published or easily available, and also excerpts from reports and discussions concerning Liberal policies. It would not have been possible to follow these procedures had it not been for the generous assistance of Lindsay Kesal and Tim Luard. Both of them were excellent 'trackers-down' of source material and showed a persistence verging on fanaticism in producing what I was looking for. Lindsay also acted as amanuensis, and must be thanked particularly for her editorial assistance.

Many academic colleagues, students and a succession of long suffering secretarial staffs at LSE, Edinburgh and York were involved as witnesses in the events I shall describe. I thank them all for their tolerance and understanding. I hope I shall be forgiven for any involuntary involvement they may have suffered in my incursions into political activity and for only mentioning by name those whose collaboration had an effect on my activities as an economic adviser.

This book is dedicated to the memory of three liberals who supported my own efforts throughout the years covered by these recorded experiences. They also remained friends long after these had gone by, for we frequently continued to discuss how the cause of liberalism, shorn of party politics, could be advanced. My debt to Jo Grimond, Graham Hutton and Frank Paish can never be fully repaid. (Some of my correspondence with Jo is now in the hands of the National Library of Scotland.)

Margaret, my wife, is inured to what happens when I put pen to paper. She has had a meagre reward in the form of reading the text but I could not let it see the light of day without her scrutiny. Slips in spelling, syntax and standpoint may remain, but these would be more in evidence were it not for her searching eye and sceptical view of my interpretation of events in our joint past. I have defied her in mentioning the part that she has played and in expressing my profound gratitude to her for giving her honest opinion of what I have written.

Finally, let me express my gratitude to Professor John Haldane for directing my steps towards Imprint Academic, thus introducing me to Anthony Freeman. Anthony's editorial advice has been invaluable alongside his skills in seeing that the manuscript is transmuted into something of publishable form. I hope his confidence in the final result is fully justified.

# Chapter 1
# *Anxious to do Good*

## I: Some Background

Those who consider policy questions related to the actions of government can be divided into two classes — at least if they are economists. There are those who regard these questions as posing an intellectual problem which can be tackled with the tools of their trade, usually some form of formal modelling. A personal attitude towards the results of the policy is not relevant or at least is suppressed. If personal emotion is involved, it lies in the 'kick' obtained from exercising professional skills, and the choice of problem studied, if a choice exists, and will be driven by the expected degree of aesthetic pleasure. In contrast, there are those who are attracted to a problem because the result of solving it accords with their judgement about whether the world will be a better place if the problem is attended to. Such a view does not conflict with a desire to give one's best as a professional economist in seeking a solution, but it is conditioned by the satisfaction derived from one's attempt 'to do good' and the opportunity cost of time spent as between cogitation and persuasion. I fall into this second category.

The choice of which approach to follow may be predetermined, to a marked extent, by family background, education and training. In Scotland, a country once traditionally associated with 'plain living and high thinking', children of professional families were always being reminded that the receipt of a secondary and university education was a privilege which carried with it some obligation to serve the community. I remember this precept being drummed into us in school morning assemblies, in church sermons and in the content of university curricula in the humanities where what were good manners, morals and policies were central to the intellectual debate. Even as profane a subject as economics, studying the 'ordinary business of life' (Alfred Marshall), was coloured by general precepts about what were the 'best' economic systems. One was invited to believe that positive economics only derived its rationale from its contribution to the 'good society'. Hence the adherence to the term 'political economy' as a more accurate description of the discipline. Unlike England, higher education was more generally available and 'bettering one's condition' (Adam Smith) through education, with the sacrifices that entailed, was a widely accepted, and highly prized, objective of poorer families.

In my youth, higher education was still adapted to the filling of posts offering opportunities for public service, not only at home but also abroad in the then colonies and Commonwealth countries. The range of opportunities was considerable, both in general teaching posts and specialised occupations such as engineering, medicine, and agriculture. As early as 1910, my father Alexander Peacock became the first government entomologist in the Colonial Service in Nigeria, studying the transmission of disease by insects. In doing so, he was exempted from the condition of an indenture system by which he had received public funding to finance his university studies on condition that he became a school teacher. No other way then was open for him to finance study for a degree.

As I write this, I realise more and more that he was a particularly hard act to follow so far as 'doing good' is concerned. Both in pre-WW1 Nigeria and during WW itself, he advanced the knowledge of the transmission of diseases and how these could be controlled by subjecting himself to being bitten by mosquitoes and infected by lice thereby contracting malaria in West Africa and later trench fever whilst serving on the Western Front.

A crucial encounter with the process of government came to many of us, if not as a surprise then certainly as a shock, when World War II broke out and we found ourselves drafted into the Armed Forces or specialist occupations where technical knowledge was required. Our parents, albeit reluctantly, laid their pacificism aside — the pledge not to see the horrors of the First World War repeated — and assumed, as we did, that the call to arms was fully justified. Perhaps it was more the herd instinct for survival rather than anxiety about doing good which led us into battle, but there can be little doubt that there formed the general expectation that our conscription was not only necessary but also an opportunity to prove ourselves worthy citizens. As the war progressed and survival seemed more than a possibility, our time horizons were pushed back causing us to consider the future and what kind of world we would encounter and what part we could play in its shape. It was perhaps surprising that we were not content with the fact that we had survived but asked the question 'survived for what?'. Or perhaps it was not so surprising to the many of us whose training (or conditioning) would now be complemented by maturity and experience which could renew the opportunity to realise our talents through some form of public service.

We were therefore willing recruits to causes centred in creating better social conditions for all, epitomised in the enthusiastic reception of the Beveridge Report, published in 1942, which offered the promise of a 'just society' made possible by universal social security. It is strange, looking back over 60 years, to remember that the same year saw the publication of what has become a much more influential work about the role of government in this process of change, namely Hayek's *The Road to Serfdom*, that devastating attack on the extension of the power of the state which then seemed to be the inevitable and acceptable consequence of adopting Beveridge's conclusions.

In fact, my own, decidedly minor, part in the debate on economic policy, which has continued to this day and fuelled my 'anxiety to do good', begins, as it did for many young economists, in how to resolve the aims of creating a society in which the constraints on individual opportunities for all were minimized with limitation to the power of the state; in other words resolving the difference, as they appeared at the time, between a Beveridgean and Hayekian view of the world. I deliberately use the language of that time, if only to demonstrate how easy it was for us to speak about these matters in slogans without getting down to the hard work of explaining what we meant. I know that it is a language often associated with priggishness, as if one had an inside track into the business of knowing what is good for others and how to attain it. Believe me, as I shall later illustrate, anyone with even a modicum of sense will soon discover that giving content to one's ideas of what are good policies and trying to have others believe that one has the capacity to translate these into proposals which can guide the acts of government will be in for a rude shock.

## II:  Sources of Advice

The sensible thing to do, so it would appear, before deciding on a career as a 'do-gooder', might be to take some advice. The only advice I feel able to give, as a result of the experiences that I shall relate, is that one learns principally from one's mistakes. Anyone in this position is like Christian in *Pilgrim's Progress* in his encounter with Mr Worldly Wiseman. His advice, it will be recalled, was for Christian not to embark on his journey at all, for the chances of success were minimal and the rewards would be meagre. However, to counter this by consulting someone more sympathetic to one's aspirations is to risk being misled by their encouragement. For the best of motives, they can be economical with the truth, for they do not wish to damp the enthusiasm of the young. They prefer to leave them to take the gamble that their luck might hold, and they will not have to encounter the common difficulties that others have faced and failed to overcome.

There is an alternative which is to seek some sort of apprenticeship to those who are already in the business of advice-giving. I can illustrate this from my own experience. A famous Scots preacher, George MacLeod, used his great gifts as an orator to urge students to help the poor. From time to time he acted as the influential agent of social settlements not only in Scotland but south of the Border, who, in wartime, wished to fill the places of male social workers conscripted into the Armed Forces. Inspired by his brand of Christian socialism I went to London with a few others at MacLeod's instigation, believing that we were to be shelter marshals helping those herded into air raid shelters with a subsidiary commitment to assist the social settlements, where we were lodged, with their social work amongst the disadvantaged. As it happened, the summer of 1941 saw a partial lull in the bombing of London, and we found that we were expected to help with less congenial and less glamorous tasks. The idea that at barely nineteen, one was equipped to explain to the youth of Bermondsey, infinitely more streetwise than oneself though only fifteen years of age, how to cope with the moral dangers resulting from their sudden affluence from their wages as clearers of bomb sites, was laughable indeed. The lesson is clear enough. The first essential for doing good must be to have some special skills and knowledge and to know how these might be applied. But what are these skills and is a university the correct place to acquire them?

Any decision was postponed by being called up into the Royal Navy (RN), and I have given account of this elsewhere.[1] Whatever I thought might be the proper course of action was now constrained by what I was ordered to do. The skills that the RN required of me were my youthful enthusiasms, my physical fitness, and enough abilities to serve as an intelligence officer coupled with a knowledge of German. I could not have predicted this, and, indeed, that, by the end of the war and with the opportunity to finish a degree in Economics and Political Science at my *Alma Mater*, St Andrews, I would have already got married and would finish my studies in 1947 with a wife and two children. Any idea of following some single guiding star chosen by one-

---

[1] See Alan Peacock, *The Enigmatic Sailor*, Whittles Publishing, 2004. I explain there how an unusual naval career further influenced my intellectual development.

self and when to set out on the journey it would define for me would be an illusion. If I was to make some sort of a stab at being involved in doing good, it had to be within the confines of developing one's talents as an economist; and the opportunity to do so had to come quickly if I was to be able to support my family. Fortunately it did, and fortunately also economics or 'political economy' still embodied a long tradition of involvement in public affairs.

This is a not unfamiliar story amongst my generation, and one which is vividly illustrated in the early career of one of the giants of economics, Alfred Marshall. Graduating in Cambridge as a Second Wrangler in 1867, he intended to become a molecular physicist, but it was because, in Keynes's words, 'Marshall was too anxious to do good', that he invested a large part of his time in learning about the real world, and it was not until 1885 that he identified himself fully with political economy when he was elected to the Chair of that name in Cambridge. The story of this transformation so fascinated Keynes, and anyone interested in the path trod by those who believe that their subject should be harnessed to the 'service of man' (to quote the sub-title of a well-known Chemistry text of the 1930s) should read Keynes's penetrating account of Marshall's conception of his own professional destiny. But this account does more; for it contains Keynes's own conclusion about the implications of Marshall's position:

> The study of economics does not seem to require any specialised gifts of an unusually high order. Is it not, intellectually regarded, a very easy subject compared with the higher branches of philosophy and pure science? Yet good, even competent, economists are the rarest of birds. An easy subject, at which very few excel! The paradox finds its explanation, perhaps, in that the master-economist must possess a rare *combination* of gifts. He must reach a high standard in several different directions and must combine talents not often found together. He must be mathematician, historian, statesman, philosopher—in some degree. He must understand symbols and speak in words. He must contemplate the particular in terms of the general, and touch abstract and concrete in the same flight of thought. He must study the present in the light of the past for the

purposes of the future. No part of man's nature or his institutions must lie entirely outside his regard. He must be
purposeful and disinterested in a simultaneous mood; as
aloof and incorruptible as an artist, yet sometimes as near
the earth as a politician …[2]

This counsel of perfection was fortunately not known to
me when I embarked on the career of economist, otherwise I
would probably have turned to simpler ways of trying to
help humanity.

### III: Who's Listening?

A question which must nag even the most naïve believer in
analytical prowess and cheerful persistence as the main
pieces of equipment in attempting to do good is how far this
will induce anyone to listen to you. Even if you are allowed
into the debate, why should you assume that you have some
monopoly of the truth in seeking ways of changing the
world for the better? The benefit of hindsight offers a
let-out. I found that there were three areas of disagreement
which have to be faced in a discourse on what is 'best' for
society. To some this may offer the prospect of resolving differences between thinkers which will result in some agreed
pattern of action which all reasonable people will accept. In
case this is regarded as fanciful, let me point out that one of
Mr Blair's favourite gurus, John MacMurray, Professor of
Moral Philosophy at Edinburgh, believed that this was not
only desirable but also possible, and when some years later
I became a young Professor of Economics at Edinburgh, I
discovered that he had set up a Social Science Research
Centre whose members consisted of social scientists from
various disciplines. Propinquity alone was expected to act
as a potent force for arriving at common truths, all being
assumed to be anxious to do good.

However, consider what is involved in this search for
some Hegelian 'higher form of unity'. One would have to
agree on the facts; for example, what the national figures
revealed, say, about economic growth and about the distri-

---

[2]    JM Keynes, 'Alfred Marshall' in *Essays in Biography*, ed. Geoffrey
Keynes, Mercury Books, London, 1933, pp. 140–41.

bution of incomes. That might just seem possible, provided one believed in the techniques used in the collection, collation and presentation of statistics. This suggests that a pre-condition of any scientific investigation in which empirical knowledge is important must be the honesty and integrity of the investigators. However, this is not enough, for, given that the resources to conduct statistical investigation, either privately or publicly financed, are bound to be limited, there will be disagreement about the order of priority as to which statistics are 'worth collecting'. Of course, the form of data collection may depend on the analytical foundations of the investigation, and be designed to reveal the trends, say, in the economic development of a country, the relative quantities of different indicators of that development and may stimulate discussion of the determinants of their movement.

There would seem to be no reason in principle that agreement could not be obtained on the mode of assessment of the analysis, which implies acceptance of the logic of scientific investigation. The great virtue of mathematical modelling which now dominates economics teaching is that it clarifies the assumptions behind the causal processes that economists try to identify. That is not to say that it is easy to agree on the assumptions themselves or on the values of the parameters in any model. If one goes further and defines the ultimate purpose of any model as that of offering a reliable guide as to what will happen if the parameters are changed, eg by some form of government action, then agreement must be reached on the appropriate tests of the reliability of the empirical estimates. The price of obtaining such agreement may be high in terms of intellectual effort and technical resources and even a robust model may not remain so for long, given the instability in the value of the parameters as a result of changing economic behaviour. But these problems point only towards the difficulties of economic modelling itself which all those party to any agreement will recognise, and not to any predisposition of any of the participants in the scientific discussion to reject the methodology of model building.

However, there are profound practical problems encountered by anyone interested in what they would regard as the 'best' course of action. Progress in economic analysis, as in all forms of scientific investigation, inevitably entails the modification, often the rejection, of previous theories and current hypotheses which do not meet the tests of viability. Where this involves attacking firmly entrenched views, well-tempered discussion according to the rules of scientific investigation can be crowded out by attempts to rely on authority as the ultimate arbiter. This may not matter much if this is a typical parochial academic pursuit confined to the pages of professional journals, but its ramifications can be considerable if major governmental policy decisions depend on it. Reputations of the great and the good may be at stake and they may be disposed to use their 'pull' to influence politicians and senior civil servants to support them. If important political decisions depend on the scientific evidence, there is no guarantee that they will have firm foundations. The problem is exacerbated if policy makers, faced with conflicting views about the scientific basis of their policy decisions, choose those which support the case which enhances their reputation. Unfortunately, this is an all too common occurrence, as I shall demonstrate later.

We come to the third problem. Agreement on what will constitute 'doing good' faces the fundamental challenge that it depends not only on agreement about facts and analysis but also about values. Scientific investigation cannot help us in the choice of policy objectives; only with the implications of accepting and implementing them. Of course, anyone, whether self-appointed or employed as an adviser on government policies, can in principle be useful in explaining the conflicts in objectives and how these might be resolved. An adviser may be able to go further and indicate the relation between different trade-offs, such as that between achieving an economic growth target alongside social security, and the degree of consensus to be achieved, if the degree of consensus is the relevant factor in being able to implement the objectives. This is what is presumed to be the case in the design of democratic systems of government, although the word 'democratic' can mean anything from mob rule engineered in vicious dictatorships to the acceptance of free voting systems with constitutional constraints against the tyranny of majority rule. The ultimate misuse of scientific investigation is that of devising techniques for ensuring support for some arbitrary system of values which accords with the wishes of some unelected group determined to grasp and to retain power.[3]

As I was to discover, doing one's best as far as one's skills allow without fear or favour is a severe test. Producing the appropriate facts and analysis for the task in hand is difficult enough. Presenting them in a form which is to be understood and cannot be distorted by those who have to consider them, whether politicians, business leaders or government officials, takes practice and patience. This entails having to 'work one's passage' with customers of economic advice who are not necessarily sold on the idea that university pedagogues are specialists in presenting ideas clearly and concisely. There is indeed much to learn from their concerns about presentation of new ideas on policy, and their use of persistent questioning to obtain acceptance of the fact that these could be more clearly expressed. In the higher civil service, as I later discovered, the word 'academic' retains its pejorative sense of 'unworldly' or 'unrealistic'. The timing of a riposte to their somewhat combative attitude had to be carefully chosen. My opportunity came when, having had it accepted that I had a contribution to make to their efforts to induce some Minister to follow sensible courses of action, I demurred at the use of the word 'academic' in criticism of some suggestions that I had offered to improve our briefing. I was challenged to epitomise the civil servants' approach to the issues facing us. To my surprise I had no difficulty in responding—the appro-

[3]    This may appear to condemn 'political economists' who follow the tradition of Adam Smith and regard rhetoric as a legitimate tool of professional discourse. Not so. It is one thing to make a case for one's own set of values and another to do so for a set of values, whether one accepts them or not, where the purpose is to have these imposed on others and no alternatives may be presented, ie competition in presentation of value systems is not permitted.

priate pejorative term is 'pragmatic'. There was laughter all round. I felt that I was now a full paid-up member of the team and, surprising to me, learned to be quicker on my feet — an additional skill, it will be noted, required of Ministers, politicians or business clients who expect instant punditry.

## IV: The Costs of Doing Good

The adventure of claiming to be able to improve the world is the first of two important moral issues. I shall only deal briefly with the first, possibly because of my own embarrassment at having to recognise the extent to which family and friends have been affected by one's missionary zeal. Anyone who has worn out shoe leather at the humble task of delivering political pamphlets to row after row of houses will know that the time costs are high; or in my case campaigning as a young man by platform speaking for Liberal local and general election candidates in isolated parts of London. Unless the family are glad to see you out of the house evenings as well as during the day, the benefits you hope to confer on your fellow human beings are bought at the cost of those expected to wait up for you to have the coffee ready when you return, footsore and weary. One should recognise that, for most of us, as Adam Smith maintained, those outside our immediate acquaintance are a kind of abstraction, or as he put it: 'Men, though naturally sympathetic, feel so little for another with whom they have no particular connection.' The assumed benefits of one's actions on the 'abstraction' are difficult enough to measure but the costs borne by those of one's immediate circle are tangible and can be considerable.[4] The moral dilemma

[4] I remember being very worried when at a tender age I was taught to sing at school Schumann's setting of Heine's famous poem, *Die Beiden Grenadiere* (The Two Grenadiers). It will be recalled that when they discover that Napoleon has been captured, one of them does not take this as a sign to go home to his starving wife and family. He must continue to support the Emperor's cause — "let them beg their bread when they hungry are, My Emperor, My Emperor, is taken!". Nowadays that is more likely to be used as an illustration of the degree of subjection of women rather than as an extreme solution to a moral dilemma.

will vary in intensity according to individual personal circumstances.

This first issue raises the dilemma of how the 'production costs' of the proposals advocated by you as their designer require the imposing of some of them on others who have a claim on your time and attention. The second concerns the costs that these proposals can impose on those who are supposed to benefit from them. It lies at the very heart of economics that any set of proposals supposedly designed to improve human welfare requires the use of resources and therefore reference to how these resources might be obtained and the identification of those expected to supply them. Of course, one solution is for you to offer to improve the lot of others by organising yourself the supply of the goods or services necessary to improve human welfare, in the expectation that you will be paid for your trouble. In other words, you seek a market solution, which does not preclude your supplying the product below cost, if you feel so inclined — but this would be a rare case beyond the normal exercise of charity towards others. The more likely case that you are interested in dealing with is one which requires collective action either of a voluntary or of a necessarily compulsory nature as with government policies.

Here there are traps for the unwary. I have to remind myself that the prime purpose of this book is to illustrate the author's experience as a Liberal Party adviser. Policies instituted by governments or their agencies are naturally presented to the world as providing great benefits. At least a semblance of honesty is manifested in a statement of the expenditure to be incurred and how it will be translated into programmes which are designed to have desirable results; and good practice requires giving the public notice of the implications of the budgetary changes implied by the programme. Acceptability may be improved by publishing the plans as a Green Paper which welcomes public discussion and the prospect that changes in them can be contemplated in the light of proposals which make them more palatable. The awkward problem for the government or its agencies is the identification of the 'opportunity cost' of the proposals, in terms of the exclusion of alternatives, such as other items of public expenditure or the restriction imposed on private spending by the requirement of extra taxation. The government or sponsoring agent has a natural desire to require those performing the difficult task of weighing costs against benefits to present their findings in the best light possible; and in extreme cases think nothing of requiring economists engaged on this task to act as 'hired guns'. As I have argued many times before, this is contrary to the ethics of professional advice-giving, and for that very reason likely to lead to loss of reputation amongst professional peers.[5] Rigging the results is simply counter-productive.

There is a more complex problem faced by the problem of measuring opportunity cost. To the extent that close attention will be paid by the government to the results and by others with an interest in tracking them, it takes a fair degree of understanding to explain why the problem of estimation is not simply an accounting one — in crude terms, work out the costs of components of the programme, tot up the figures and, hey presto, the result is clear. Even one simple aspect of the estimation process illustrates the problem of closing the understanding gap. If a programme involves the production of benefits, lasting twenty five years ahead, the true costs will not be measured simply by aggregating the expenditure over the chosen period, for that assumes that a pound spent now is regarded as the exact equivalent of a pound spent at a later date. The nature and distribution of costs and benefits will depend on their incidence and the reaction of those affected by the programme. A new motorway may directly benefit those who prefer quicker transport and may reduce accidents, but the environmental effects may be perceived as adverse; and so on. The economist faced with carrying out the cost-benefit equation and the values in its parameters is unlikely to gain friends in the process. Moreover, intellectual honesty requires that he points out the uncertainties surrounding any calculation.

[5]    As an example, see 'The Utility Maximising Government Economist: a Comment' in Alan Peacock, *The Political Economy of Economic Freedom*, Edward Elgar, Cheltenham, 1997

The politician will be upset if his pet scheme is not sanctified by a positive result to the calculation, and those whose job it is to crawl over the economic analysis may accuse the economist of cowardice or incompetence if there is a failure to come to a definite conclusion. Keynes's famous adage: 'better to be vaguely right than precisely wrong' is good professional advice and will be subscribed to by your peer group, but following it out in the world of advice-giving is not for the thin-skinned.

### V: The Final Treason?

In TS Eliot's play *Murder in the Cathedral*, there is a famous soliloquy in which Thomas à Becket questions whether in seeking martyrdom he is not committing the 'greatest treason' of 'doing the right deed for the wrong reason'. Those who seek to do good, it is claimed, do not achieve their aim unless it is purified of any suggestion that there is personal profit to be gained from it. Doing good precludes doing well.[6] It is a particular characteristic of British attitudes to business once strongly entrenched in our ancient universities that doing good can only be associated with good causes which are managed by non-profit organisations, including government. This presupposes the adoption of a view of human nature which takes it as axiomatic that those who pursue profit as a goal are morally inferior to those who pursue other aims. Today it is reflected in what appear to be successful attempts to change the whole structure of corporate governance in order to give representation to decision making to several groups of 'stakeholders'.

This is a complex matter which will emerge time and time again in the later text. What constitutes 'good' and who is

---

[6]  I recall puzzling over a cartoon in the *New Yorker* some years ago, before it dawned on me what the joke was. A solemnly dressed 17th-century gentleman was leaning over the side of a ship like the *Mayflower* explaining to a companion that he expected in a new life in America to begin by preaching the Gospel to the pagan Indians but hoped eventually to finish up in the real estate business. It took me a little time to realise that this was a humorous manifestation of the well-known US quip that: "The Quakers came to America to do good, and finished up doing well"!

'doing well', how far one depends on the other, and how they are to be achieved are questions that have so far only been dealt with here indirectly. And once working definitions are discovered, any attempt to provide empirical evidence which would confirm or deny whether good is being done and how much, and who has or has not done well in the process produces a minefield of speculation as to the meaning of the results. There cannot be any presumption that institutional arrangements will determine whether or not individuals will act in a manner directed towards 'doing good'. The stronger version of this proposition is that it applies whether or not the employing organisation has written into its constitution and in its associated Mission Statement that it is designed to operate 'in the public interest', ie is obliged to further the 'public weal', or is more directly concerned with maximising its return to its 'stakeholders', in our subsequent narrative the members of a political party.

# Chapter 2

# The Market for Economic Advice

### I: Beginners Please

I graduated in Economics and Political Science at the University of St Andrews in 1947, and was appointed Lecturer in Economics there. My duties were primarily to give some lectures to First Year students on price theory and also to take some tutorials for Honours Students. I also gave ten lectures to medical graduates on The Economics of the Social Services as part of their training to be awarded a Diploma in Public Health, which induced me later to write extensively on the Economics of Social Policy. But my research commitments remained unspecified and the likelihood that my advice on economic questions would be sought by anyone never occurred to me.

After I had been about six months into the job, I was asked by a neighbour of mine, a young man like myself, if I would give him a piece of advice to help him in his task as a Planning Officer for Fife County Council. He was helping to prepare a Development Plan for Fife, and wished to know if it was reasonable to assume that the small town of Strathmiglo would still have a steel foundry there in twenty years time, which would employ 30 men as at present. I was taken aback, for, in the course of amplification of his task, it became clear that he was involved in what was in effect a long-term economic plan for the county, and in detail sufficient to be able to specify the size, economic structure and social conditions even for individual villages. The final product of this plan was supposed to offer clear guidance to the Planning Department on the housing 'needs' of the county. He pointed out that this procedure was being widely adopted throughout Scotland.

It is more obvious today, after the manifest failures of a succession of schemes of this kind and of the notorious National Plan of the 1960s, what was wrong with this whole approach. We cannot blame him for having to subscribe to the then widely-held belief that war-time planning, with its extensive use of physical controls, would continue to be the template for economic policies designed to influence the allocation and distribution of physical and human resources. I pointed out that, even if the government operated a Soviet-type system, there were major uncertainties about making predictions at a global level, far less in the detailed form that he required. Moreover, his whole approach neglected the possibility that individual workers were likely to be responsive to economic forces which led them to change occupation and location, and it was unlikely that government would want to or even could force them to do otherwise in the interests of plan fulfilment. Above all, where and from whom could he obtain the necessary demographic data which would govern estimates of the amount and type of housing? It turned out that this would be based on forecasts of population by the local authorities. I missed a trick by not realising at the time that such authorities were not likely to offer a scenario in which there was any suggestion that the population in their area could possibly fall!

Not surprisingly, my neighbour was distressed and both of us probably made a mental note that the other's profession was bogus. Some years later, Sir Arnold Plant told me of a similar instance at a much more grandiose level of planning discussion. His views were greeted by a Treasury official with the angry comment: 'you economists spread a fog around wherever you go', to which he replied: 'that's the natural result of the injection of cold air into hot'!

My scepticism was in line with a good deal of the economic advice that I have given or have scrutinized—that economists are practised at providing negative, albeit often sound, advice — what not to do when uncertainty surrounds the estimates on which some project is based. Coming up with a clear and positive statement which offers convincing evidence for some definite course of action by the client is much more difficult. The difficulty increases the more he or she expects to make decisions where an economist can add to their knowledge. For example, there are few economists that I could trust to tell me how to maximize the returns on my small cache of liquid assets. 'Since you know all about the stock market, why aren't you rich?' is the loaded question put to me on several occasions by sceptical tycoons. Usually, my reply is that you do not hire a ballistic expert in order to learn how to play tennis. Some then admit that the perspective of the 'ballistic expert' may be worth a consultation.

## II: Barriers to Entry into the Advice Business

This experience did have one positive effect. It spurred my first attempt to define the agenda, being primarily concerned with the application of political economy to policy questions. Such a desire was already embedded in my mind. One of the requirements for obtaining a joint Honours Degree in Political Economy and Political Science was to write a thesis and I chose as subject: *The Optimum Theory of Population*. Policy interest would be covered by having to show how the theory had formed the basis of economic appraisals of population growth and their effect on government policies. There had been considerable debate about the welfare effects of population change by British economists, after Malthus — still the most famous name in the economics of population. In the first three decades of the 20th century, prominent British economists such as Pigou, Beveridge, Keynes, Dennis Robertson, and Edwin Cannan had contributed to a running debate on the causes and consequences of population change. The debate itself, initially concerned about the question whether or not the UK was 'over-populated', had switched dramatically in the late 1930s, as a consequence of fears that the long-run prospect for the UK was that of a declining population. It has long since been forgotten that one of the most influential post-war reports affecting social policy was that of the Royal Commission on Population (1949), although family allow-ances had already been introduced in 1945. The debate continues, but now on a world-wide basis and occasionally I have been tempted to take part in it, finding my now-dog-eared thesis a useful reminder of the issues.

Inevitably the thesis was a jejeune attempt to deal with a very difficult set of issues, but at least offered some sem-blance of scholarship and appreciation of how to present ideas. The circumstance of its preparation, however, warned me of one of the principal hurdles in handling policy questions — how to assimilate material and assess its quality, and place this activity in the context of a time con-straint with a deadline for the emergence of the 'finished product'. Students nowadays expect to be given a good start in such matters with instruction on source material and how to download it through their laptops. They become prac-tised in giving instructions to the genii bottled up in their computers who undertake the rough work of correcting the spelling (and even the grammar) and paragraphing of their work, not to speak of performing miracles of computation and statistical analysis.

The student will expect, indeed may be expected to demand, indications of the extent to which they are on the right track and guidance from academic staff on how to keep to it. Of course, the other side of the coin is that the stu-dent will now be expected to reach a much higher standard of visual presentation, if not cogitation, than hitherto. All this has turned the reading rooms of university libraries where silence used to be enforced into vast stables of screen searching 'scholars' whose keyboard facilities collectively emit a sound like muffled horses' hooves. The more lenient librarians (now known as 'knowledge directors') in charge of reading rooms (sorry, work stations) allow users to bring in their lunch with the statutory plastic bottle of water. (No doubt there are examples of those who permit students to call up a takeaway on their mobile phones to deliver them a meal.)

I imagined that as a new, if very junior, member of staff I would have access to some secretarial facilities, and receive the benefit of advice of more experienced colleagues. However, I have to remember that I am talking of over sixty years ago when technical facilities alone were very limited — when access to sources meant painstaking searches through catalogues, when very few university staff possessed and could use a typewriter, when few departments, other than those with access to outside financing, had secretaries and typists, far less with special skills in presenting data, when working seminars and collaborative projects were made difficult if departments were small and teaching duties for junior staff could be onerous. Not surprisingly, the acquisition of the time and skills to be both conversant with the contributions to policy questions likely to be of interest, and to be recognized as someone with something to be listened to, was going to be difficult when there were important barriers to entry to be surmounted, other than the obvious ones of youth and inexperience.

I received no advice about my thesis from any of my teachers. However, I had a running argument with Sir D'Arcy Thompson, that great polymathic figure, when I declined to support his argument that the growth in human populations must inevitably follow Malthusian patterns, as the great Darwin himself had maintained. He was then in his eighties and I was scarcely 25, and amazed to be taken seriously and listened to — an object lesson which one, now in old age, must never forget. The situation was no better when I became a junior lecturer. Our Professor had many preoccupations, notably in university politics and keeping down his golf handicap below 5, but he was a pleasant and in other ways most helpful person.

My fellow lecturers were only too glad, like myself, to have survived military service, and indeed one of them had been a prisoner of war for close on five years. They were surprised and gratified to have survived and their immediate ambition was to make up for lost youth. One of them, John

Henderson, was an exception and did respond to a wish to talk about economic analysis. Like me, he beat a retreat, and at a relatively advanced age, to become a graduate student, took a Harvard PhD, and had a very respectable career as an academic teacher and later as a member of the Congressional economics staff. I had more in common with two ex-service students, Pelcynski, to become later a philosophy don at Oxford, and Wheelwright, like myself already married, a huge giant of a man who emigrated to Australia, where he became a radical Marxist and adviser to trade unions. They wanted to know about Keynes and forced me to expound my views on Keynesian approaches to policy, though the subject was almost proscribed in our Political Economy department. But my main prop was the recently appointed Lecturer in Politics, Graeme Moodie, with degrees from both St Andrews and Oxford (PPE) and already a friend, and who had actually joined the Liberal Party and had met, and knew personally through Oxford contacts, several of its leaders. He saved me from intellectual isolation as well as keeping me abreast with liberal political thought. Later we were both foundation professors, Graeme in politics and I in economics, at the new University of York, but by then his experience and intellect lead him leftwards and he stood, if unsuccessfully, as a Labour candidate for Parliament in the 1950s.

I would not like to give the impression that I was consumed by dissatisfaction and unable to control an innate tendency to be rebellious and outspoken. Teaching duties came first and there was much to learn about presenting and explaining economics to those who had no previous knowledge of it and likely to be sceptical of much of it, and this alone required making up for extensive gaps in one's knowledge. Even then, I was the unconscious innovator, being the first lecturer who issued students with an outline of the lectures—some on subjects that he barely knew about!—in typewritten form and with a bibliography. In so doing, I required the services of a typist with access to copying facilities, and the Department possessed neither the person nor the machinery. I consulted my father who had the inestimable quality of being a favourite with junior staff because he was always kind and considerate to them. The secretary of the university Extra-Mural Department willingly responded to his request for her to help me out. But I had set a bad precedent, for there were members of staff who still wasted lecturing time by laboriously writing out their syllabus on the blackboard before turning towards their audience and lecturing, sometimes dictating, the lectures themselves.

I worked hard, realising that professional respect would require me to write contributions of article length or less, that would be acceptable to a prestigious academic journal which was 'peer-reviewed'. In contrast, the long tradition of writing one's *Meisterstuck* as a large tome, displaying wide reading and commentary on one's forbears, still prevailed north of the Border. However, the goal of finding a niche in the economics profession was a long way ahead and the current problem was choosing one's specialism, a matter which still puzzles me today and was counter, so it seemed, to the, perhaps naïve, desire 'to do good'. The short term must dominate so that I could keep my family by keeping my job. But this led me away from the dark paths through the forests of scholarly tomes in the Library which attracted me because of my rather unusual interest in earlier German economic thought towards the business of finding an extra £100 above my salary in order to pay the rent. This came my way by that invitation to give ten lectures on the economic and social problems of the social services, notably health and housing, to the Graduate Diploma in Public Health (DPH) in University College, Dundee.

I enjoyed the assignment. At times St Andrews seemed as if in a fairy tale like that of the ghostly township in the German folk-tale about Germelshausen, or latterly in the musical Brigadoon, and a weekly visit for a term to a bustling grimy city such as Dundee was a welcome contrast. (The tide of appreciation usually flowed the other way and those St Andrews-based lecturers obliged to lecture regularly in the Dundee portion of the university seemed united in their regarding it as an ordeal. But I had been reared in and retain an affection for what had long been my home town.)

The students were receptive, my own age and even older as they, too, included ex-service men, but expected me to know my stuff. I became fascinated by the evolution of the welfare state and its problems, and made an invaluable investment in a knowledge of 'national income and social accounting', the necessary institutional background to the study of government policies. But the explanation of the 'anatomy' of the economy and the place of social services in it hardly satisfied their desire to know why their development raised such controversy. For them, it seemed obvious that the optimal expenditure on health services was not an issue, and that both the advancement of medical knowledge and the availability of its results to provide universal benefits in the form of medical services for all was an absolute. Within the constraints of a short lecture course, how was I to give them some basic knowledge of economics? In the end I concentrated on the 'opportunity cost' problem that all governments have to confront which created problems for an argument that simply assumed the illimitable nature of the optimal expenditure on health. With limitations on what government could spend, and competing claims for resources, based on similar arguments to their own, by educationists, housing experts and supporters of universal social security, the 'cost' of health services had to be measured in terms of alternatives foregone.

It is surprising how this simple and obvious point comes as a revelation (usually as a rude shock) to those with special skills and interests which they believe need financial support transcending that for other services. It is not so surprising when one considers the implications of accepting it. Given limited resources for health services, this leaves the suppliers of health services with their own opportunity cost problem of how to achieve a 'proper' allocation between alternative services. In the enthusiasm to establish a National Health Service, an answer sought in the expression of patients' choice and their purse was regarded as the worst solution. One based on political and expert medical opinions traded on the acceptance of an electorate who were willing to be told what was good for them. But then the medical services actually to be provided were in the play of bargaining between medical specialists themselves and between them and government bureaucrats. With the best will in the world, and the desire to improve the health and welfare of patients, patients' needs could not be based on some recognisable objective assessment, but on an uneasy professional consensus, which was liable to change in the light of medical advances and actual experience of working within a central planning framework.

I did not have the knowledge or confidence at the time to express my views in this form and there was little empirical support then available to back up the economic analysis of health services, which has latterly become an enormously important branch of applied economics, widely recognized as of practical use. (I was later closely involved in its development.) The opportunity cost point did appear to impress on the students that problems of choice would be something that would hit them when they became part of the NHS hierarchy. One or two students recalled that they had been lectured to in the Services by those who claimed that in the kind of economy of the 1930s, the free market was characterized by under-employment of resources. Would that not mean that governments could remedy this situation, and would not government expenditure have to be devoted to removal of gross inequalities be a means for remedying a general economic problem. (In other words, the opportunity cost of an NHS of the kind envisaged would be zero!) I rather fudged the issue, being neither fully competent nor able to offer a digest of Keynesian economics in the one lecture sessions that might be spared for a reply — a subjective judgment about the opportunity cost of doing so measured in terms of the lecture subjects I would have to discard! I simply referred them to the Labour Government's own expectations that the immediate post-war problem would be characterized by the need to find enough productive resources to repair the damage of war and the public's desire to be compensated for the sacrifices that war had entailed. I did however point out that the social services did embody methods for making up any short-fall in demand for available resources which might arise in the future. This might be done by the power to vary national insurance contributions as a means of altering income levels or by schemes for increasing public investment when expected total demand would not be sufficient to prevent under-employment of resources. I blush with shame and can hardly bring myself to retail this crude response. One's pedagogic history becomes punctuated by the memories of covering up one's ignorance by a dubious answer to an unexpected question, particularly if one has not gained sufficient confidence to admit one's ignorance.

### III: Looking Elsewhere

Looking back to 60 years ago sets traps for the memory. Apart from natural decay, it becomes selective, notably in the process of editing so that the revelations of one's past errors are excised or minimized. Exaggerating one's foresight is a common example, a product of both the leaks in the box of memory and the influence of one's vanity on the selection process itself. The fear is that in not using these presentational tricks, the honest result can be of little interest to the reader.

I might get away with the impression that my mind was so focused on the desire to 'do good' that I was already of a mind to devote my professional life to solving the riddle of what was then known as 'the clash between social security and economic progress', recalling the title of the then influential book by Alan Loveday. No, I had not yet traced any connection between the hard work of preparing lectures for intelligent young doctors about the economic background to the growing welfare state and how I could use my knowledge for the 'benefit of humanity', an objective itself redolent of ambiguity. What I did realize was that this might be an area of research that would interest me very much, only rivalled then by the ferret-like lust for penetrating the contents of those dusty, neglected tomes of 19th-century

German economists languishing in the darker corners of the St Andrews University Library basement, unread and not much cared for. This common disease of academic foraging remained with me all my academic life, but I already saw problems of relating it to the necessity of supporting a family. Perhaps when I had done good and also done reasonably well I could afford the luxury of penetrating the minds of the giants on whose shoulders we stood, although one soon found out that there were dangers in doing so if they turned out to have feet of clay.

It was clear to me that there was one thing I must do, and soon, given that I was now approaching 26, untested and untried. I must look for a post elsewhere, and not 'capitulate to the amenities' of St Andrews, with all its charm and prestige. (The phrase appears in the Inaugural Lecture of the first incumbent of the Chair of Political Economy, James Wilkie Nisbet, in his time a well known amateur golfer.) My policy interests were too closely bound up with political life and with those closely affected by the permeation of state regulation of their economic activities. Above all, I needed to have the stimulus and interchange of ideas with the like-minded and committed, both economists and their 'subject-matter'. I sought—and found—just the opportunity to grasp, though not without qualms of doubt about my capacity to fill its remit. This brings me nearer to the kernel of the process of bringing one's professional expertise, such as it is, to bear on policy matters. How far my expectations were realized is the subject of the next chapter.

Chapter 3

# Chance and Circumstance

## I: Goodbye St Andrews

To the delight of Margaret, who had encouraged me to apply, and to the surprise of her family and mine, I was appointed to a Lectureship in Economics at the London School of Economics and Political Science (LSE) to take up post in October 1948. I have always maintained that my inquisitors, who included Professors Robbins, Hayek, Sayers, Phelps Brown, Meade and Paish, had an exaggerated respect for Scots higher education, apparently confirmed by the fact that someone of my generation who had studied German economic thought and was assumed to have a deep knowledge and respect of Adam Smith, was rather unusual. I sensed it was Frank Paish and James Meade who led Lionel Robbins and Friedrich Hayek away from testing my knowledge of the history of economic thought, conscious of the fact that LSE needed, and quickly, someone able to give an elementary economics course to students training to become social workers and who were notoriously resistant to economic ideas. As explained earlier, I had given such a course at St Andrews, and had lectured to young doctors taking a diploma in public health who needed to know something about the welfare state. I never enquired from these notable figures why I was appointed in preference to fizzers like Frank Hahn, but there I was with a job in my lap with a small rise in salary at the princely sum of £600 per annum, payable monthly, a welcome change from being paid three-monthly in arrears at my *Alma Mater*.

In a relatively small community of academics, as St Andrews was at the time, the swapping of a post encrusted with the prestige of Scotland's oldest university for one at a small specialised college scarcely fifty years old did not pass unnoticed. It was the occasion of concern about how far one could cope with the moral temptations of what one colleague called 'the benighted South'. A prominent divine wished me well by remarking that I may have sold my soul to the devil, for LSE was 'an awfie wicked place'. The Professor of German, a former lecturer at Bedford College, London, warned me that I had taken a step downwards, for college lecturers in London did not have university lecturer status. Surprisingly, our local Minister seemed out of line in expressing doubts about the suitability of transferring to membership of the congregation of the Church of Scotland in London and regarded the Episcopal Church a much more suitable source of spiritual comfort. But James Wilkie Nisbet, Professor of Political Economy, although offering me the prospect of rapid promotion if I stayed, understood a desire to see if one's wings would spread, and indicated that he would welcome my return at some later stage of my career. He may have been somewhat glad to be rid of a difficult customer but our common liberal sympathies strengthened a desire to remain friends. After a confusing and exhausting series of efforts to find somewhere to live, we settled with our few possessions in North Finchley in the autumn of 1948.

## II: Unsettling Settling In

It was no surprise to find that LSE was an altogether different academic institution but one could hardly anticipate the associated shock of becoming one of its members who had no previous experience of its ethos and practices. One expected that part of that ethos was an intellectual liberalism shared by scholars with very different political and philosophical views, and so it turned out, at least during the period of my tenure (1948–56). What was more difficult to contend with was the expectation that those appointed to lecturing posts and above were already fully capable of participation not only in the teaching of their subject but also of contributing to its development. This might suggest that rugged individualism was already built into one's make-up and that professional progress would be characterised by both the desire and the capability to survive strong competition. Certainly, from the very beginning of one's tenure, there was an emphasis on leaving one to find one's own feet with one consulted about what one was to teach but no indication as to how it should be taught—it was assumed you knew! I remember that I went to Lionel Robbins with an outline of my general course for students of social policy and social work, under the impression that I required his sanction, and he was initially puzzled before realising that I had been working under a more hierarchical system of academic governance. 'Alan,' he said, "I am always willing to tender advice, if you think I can, but approval is not mine to give. This is liberty hall.' (I have met people who simply do not believe that Lionel Robbins, though professing liberal ideas, was other than a patrician establishment figure with whom one was expected to agree, but that is certainly not my experience of him and I was a lucky person to have become his colleague and to have enjoyed his friendship for forty years.)

However, there was intense competition of ideas presented in graduate and staff seminars, but also sufficient of a collective interest in helping one another, especially amongst junior staff with their feet on the bottom of the ladder, by exchange of ideas, sometimes leading to joint research work and publication. Individualism was tempered with a desire to avoid being forced into a solipsist state. This meant learning not to be afraid of your colleagues finding out that you had large patches of ignorance in your intellectual make-up which might lead you to talk and write nonsense. The first lesson for living in such a society of scholars is to be able to accept criticism not only from one's peers but from one's pupils, and to select from it how you might improve your knowledge and skills.

I fondly imagined that I should be able to hold my own in academic conversation on the passing show of contemporary economic events. Certainly there was ample opportunity to obtain practice in doing so in the course of morning coffee or at the lunch table, and given the mix of disciplines claiming expertise in and often participation in the events themselves. But if this was an expectation fulfilled and confirmation of the sagacity of having successfully applied for a post at LSE, it was something of another rude shock as well. I soon discovered that I knew nothing, or nothing which entitled me to consider that anyone should bother to listen to me.

The range of knowledge displayed and confident judgements delivered by my new colleagues was a formidable barrier to participation. I hardly knew enough to have the confidence to admit ignorance and at least then be worth encouraging to ask pertinent questions which would allow the practised hands to expand on their views. That seemed to be the traditional function of the tenderfoot intellectuals and those joining the staff from the ranks of LSE graduates were already well aware of their role as well as having the advantage of being familiar with the views of those of their mentors who were now their senior colleagues.

Of course, I did have some experience of mortification at the extraordinary range of knowledge, confidently expressed, by 'les grandes hommes', as St Andrews had several of international consequence, but the daily 'causeries' were not their milieu of disquisition. They seemed to be more comfortable delivering, as it were, 'sermons from the pulpit', carefully honed and less tuned to immediate events, with the physical barrier of a raised platform and the psychological one of hard seats for their listeners and the formal atmosphere of the lecture hall; clearly not a favourable environment for informal debate. Some years later little seemed to have changed. When I took up my first professorial appointment at Edinburgh in 1957, I invited Harry Johnston, then at Manchester, to give a seminar on international trade policy. I found that Edinburgh offered no money for finance of professional seminars but had plenty for public lectures, the spread of knowledge being considered more important, it seemed, than seeking to advance one's subject. Harry obliged with a splendid extempore lecture interspersed with regular clicking noises emanating from chewing matchsticks to curb his irresistible desire to chain smoke. That fascinated his respectful audience, but they were appalled when he called for questions at the end of his lecture, his answers to them being devastatingly critical of his questioners' naivety. My own attempt gained me the compliment that the analysis I applied was correct but that the example I gave was rubbish. Fancy! He had criticised, of all people, the Professor and in front of his own students! Those who knew Harry will realise that I had come out of the exchange rather better than most!

### III: Further Uncomfortable Comparisons

There was another significant difference in the nature of informal discussion at the LSE compared to St Andrews. The 'stars' were not only practised in the art of practical cogitation but based their knowledge of current affairs on personal knowledge and often friendship with influential public figures, and on a continuous basis, and might themselves fall into this category. This gave a very different focus on how aspiring economists and social scientists might approach the study of contemporary society, for those who would judge our performance as academics would be bound to be influenced by their closeness to events and to those who sought to control them. For example, a good practical result of propinquity of these scholars to their subject matter was their willingness to reduce the costs of access to the decision making processes in government and business to their junior colleagues which their place in the 'network' permitted. I was to benefit immensely in this regard, as will be clear later.

But with the benefits of a Scots education that had led to my appointment, did I not have an immense advantage of being well supplied with intellectual capital as well as the growing self-confidence conferred by surviving four years of danger and hardship as a 'former naval person'? The latter experience, as it did for a number of other new members of staff, made one likely to be more self-assured and less impressed by any form of pomposity. I soon found that my stock of intellectual capital was too heavily cluttered up with 'curious learning' — to use an epithet I once heard a High Court judge employ as characteristic of economists' evidence as expert witnesses. The second element in the shock of personal assimilation as a colleague was provided by the readiness of new junior staff, particularly those educated at LSE, not only to know how to act as respectable 'feeds' to induce our seniors to reveal their great thoughts and experiences, but also how to participate in any ensuing debate.

It was not simply a question of having the confidence to admit ignorance but also of their thorough grasp as how to use their analytical training in trying to advance the argument. The example which comes to mind is that of the intense debate at the time on how nationalised industries should be organised. I imagined that any Common Room discussion would be centred in how they could be organised efficiently, and thought I might know enough from being a regular reader of *The Economist*. Before giving voice in any such discussion I thought I might derive enlightenment from an impending seminar just arranged between Cambridge, LSE and Oxford economists to be held over a weekend. The introductory papers mystified me because they relied on the presentation of formal models, obviously totally familiar to my confreres but not to me, which 'proved' the validity of the 'golden rule' of marginal cost pricing of the nationalised industries' products, instead of the *simpliste* view that they should 'cover their average costs'. The nice piece of economists' sleight of hand in this elegant presentation is that it indicated that there could be cases where the optimal price of the product should be zero! Even more impressive than the models was the percolation of this argument in Common Room discussion and skilful translation of the rule into a form to aid the understanding of non-economist members of staff. Like me, the experts in public administration were sceptical of the whole idea, but I could hardly take their part, particularly as I had then little idea about the detail of nationalised industries' costs structures. Many years later, this argument still penetrated the discussion of the economics of broadcasting, but by then I had long since seen through the hidden assumptions in the model which torpedoed any attempt to apply the 'rule' in anything like its original formulation.

I was initially uncomfortable because there was no way to prevent exposing my ignorance as I would be expected to participate in graduate and staff seminars in which one's performance or lack of it would soon become manifest, not to speak of lecturing to undergraduates specialising in Economics who probably knew much more than I did. Of course, I was underestimating the perceptiveness and understanding of my new senior colleagues who made full allowance, perhaps too much, for the adjustment problems facing ex-service personnel. However, it seemed better not to assume that one should take them into one's confidence about the trauma of adjustment. I was not in any case given to weeping on anyone's shoulder, and that itself might be taken as evidence enough of their having not been sold a pup.

### IV: Good Advice

I did indulge in one minor fishing expedition by asking Lionel Robbins about possible future research. Characteristically, he took me to the Reform Club and, having put me at ease with a congenial lunch, we sat down in one of its capacious lounges and I put it to him that perhaps I should capitalise on my knowledge of German literature and write a critical study of von Mangoldt's pathbreaking work in price theory and then submit the results for a PhD. The latter suggestion he rejected, making me even more concerned for he said that someone of my knowledge and experience did not have to prove himself by a further piece of paper. Although himself a strong believer that a necessary condition for being a good economist was to be conversant with the history of the subject, he warned me that, although the choice was mine, the breadth of scholarship needed to produce a thesis in economic thought would compete with the prospect of producing something more quickly and expertly in the analytical economics applicable to current economic policy problems that clearly interested me. To put it crudely in economic parlance, not to be attributed to Lionel, I have to add, a thesis in economic thought would represent a long-term investment with uncertain professional returns, compared to short term investments based on sharpening up one's existing skills which could produce work more likely to command professional attention. I was not sure that I had got the answer that should satisfy me, though grateful for his views, and it was only some years later that I realised what good advice it was and its hidden implications. Anyone seriously interested in the history of the subject may have a better understanding of its importance, the more they attempt to emulate the great figures in its past. But one thing was clear. I must work hard at 'sharpening up my skills' and find a subject to test them on.

# Chapter 4

# *Fast Tracking to Policy*

## I: Introduction: Journey into the Unknown

Following my lunch with Lionel Robbins, alongside hours spent on familiarising myself with modern texts on analytical economics and its mathematical foundations, I decided to combine this with building on a previous knowledge and interest in social policy. The economic aspects of reconciling the growth and stability of the economy with an active policy of increasing economic and social opportunities, notably to reduce the incidence of poverty, seemed a theme very much in accordance with my political beliefs at the time. Not only that. It was a hot topic in contemporary political discussion particularly when it was becoming clear that the assumptions on which some of the major proposals, such as the Beveridge Plan and the National Health Service, were based might not be fulfilled. For an economist to be able to say anything useful on these matters rested on a detailed study of the statistical framework now being developed as the basis of understanding how government policies influence the structure of the economy and an analysis of the reaction to these policies by those whose actions they were designed to influence.

I began by a literature trawl through the professional economics journals and was surprised to find how little had been written on these subjects. As recorded later, over a period of thirty years from 1925 to 1955, what was then regarded in the UK as the premier journal in Economics, *The*

*Economic Journal,* published over 1,000 articles and memoranda of which only 10 concerned the social services, and only 2 of these had appeared after World War II, when the debate on social policy was at it height. It can safely be said that other prestigious journals in the UK displayed a similar position. This engendered mixed feelings—perhaps there was something inherently complex and difficult compared with other branches of applied economics which I had not appreciated; or, there was an opportunity here to fill the gap.

I remembered that when I read the Beveridge Report I was puzzled by its elaborate defence of the concept of 'insurance' and the apparent need to justify the position that his comprehensive 'national insurance' meant combining the principle of the individual paying for income protection during periods of unemployment, sickness and disability while account must be taken of the means of the insurees. Moreover, by 1948 it was clear that the Labour Government had rejected any form of involvement of voluntary bodies, such as the Friendly Societies, in the administration of the scheme which was to be entirely state-run. The collectivisation of the system to this extent contradicted the requirement of claiming that there was anything left which subscribed to the insurance principle. At most, it might be a useful marketing device to soften the blow that the finance of national insurance required its extension to the entire working population, bringing in millions of new contributors, now required by law to pay weekly employee contribution. (This recalls the US economist's remark that the 'use of the term insurance was a stroke of promotional genius'.)

There had been some questioning of the insurance principle before now, notably in James Meade's *pièce d'occasion* entitled *Planning and the Price Mechanism,* which was one of some important reminders that war-time economic policies would not be desirable or feasible to pursue under post-war conditions. However, nobody seemed to have investigated in any depth the translation of the concept of national insurance into its financial counterpart which presumably could be extracted from government accounts. I saw the prospect of writing something with both analytical and topical interest about the structure of national insurance finance, and possibly on the whole question of the scheme's role in any policy of the state's role in influencing the distribution of income.

## II:  Falling on One's Feet

I set to work and soon re-discovered my hunting instincts in flushing out references in official documents and articles which I had already employed in an amateur fashion in writing my MA thesis. (This is a common academic substitute for the more glamorous and once prestigious pastimes such as chasing foxes or shooting grouse which require more manly skills and much greater financial resources than most academics appear to command. Exceptions are so unusual as to attract widespread attention.) Fortunately the LSE library had a stock of official reports and helpful library staff and the result was that within three months I had perused, digested and harvested the products of over twenty documents ranging from Ministerial statements and parliamentary committee reports to government accounts. I had met a range of government officials, some working under Dickensian conditions in poky offices up dark passageways located off such thoroughfares as Chancery Lane and Whitehall, most of whom were very helpful, and sometimes intrigued, as in the case of the Secretary of the National Debt Commissioners, at my interest in the minutiae of their daily concerns. Such was the exhausting consequence of not finding secondary sources, such as an already extensive literature—which I have shown did not exist—which would have allowed one to ride on the back of one's colleagues or at least to find a readymade bibliography of useful references.

The upshot was an article ('The National Insurance Funds', *Economica*, August 1949) which was accepted for publication more or less as I had submitted it, survived the scrutiny of Frank Paish but was very much improved by his helpful comments and suggestions. (I was unaware that he

was the son of Sir George Paish, and, like his father, one of
the few highly regarded independent economic advisers of
the Liberal Party.) I was curious why my piece had so
quickly found a place in a top professional journal, and he
indicated why. It fitted well with the LSE tradition that the
provision of the institutional background of economic institutions was justified primarily in order to select the tools of
economic analysis that would throw light on how they
worked. Apart from Paish himself, the work of other senior
figures at LSE such as Richard Sayers' analysis of banking,
and Coase on public enterprises could be held up as examples. It produced fresh information on the financing of
national insurance, and particularly on how investment of
surpluses was carried out, but under the firm control of The
Treasury. It was topical but raised policy issues which
would be likely to remain well to the fore for years to come,
particularly in emphasising that the National Insurance
Scheme was becoming an engine of redistribution policy,
and therefore was bound to have to be closely integrated
with the fiscal system. It took me some time to realise that I
was about to become engaged in a debate that would take
me directly into the difficult terrain where economics and
politics confront one another.

   In those days, professional academic economic journals
were still regarded as a primary source of material for commentators on the contemporary economic situation, not
only quoted in business reports sent to banking and investment clients and shareholders but also in the weekly periodicals specialising in current affairs and even reached the
leader pages of the daily broadsheets. (Nowadays, only a
select few economic commentators in the mould, perhaps,
of a Samuel Brittan or Martin Wolf, would know their way
round professional journals. I recall that in my time at LSE,
the well known Professor of Sociology, Tom Marshall,
announced one day in the early 1950s that, after many years,
he was stopping taking the *Economic Journal*. (He could
accept that he could no longer understand the text of its
articles, but he drew the line at not being able even to understand their titles!)

My article was referred to in several broadsheets and by a number of professional colleagues, notably Ursula Hicks, the well known Oxford authority on public finance who, apparently characteristically, simply knocked on my door when paying a visit to LSE and sat down to explain what she could accept and what she was more sceptical about in my argument. (I came in time to owe her a great deal by way of encouragement, advice and some well deserved criticisms.) The Economic Research Council, traditional guardians of the famous 'single tax on land' philosophy, asked for permission to reprint part of it and paid me a fee for doing so. Apart from my economics colleagues, who assumed that I had simply performed as was expected (and I had not expected to do!), the practically-minded lady lecturers in social policy, notably Nancy Seear, were pleased to find an economist who had some knowledge of their concerns; and this was to have important consequences. I was naturally pleased—and relieved! At last, I could claim to be something of a professional economist.

### III: The Peacock Spreads its Wings (a little!)

Typically, it so happened, one immediate effect was on my teaching commitments. I was now to undertake supervision of graduate students writing MSc dissertations, and even a PhD student, because of my apparent expertise on matters of the finance of the welfare state which was of particular interest to overseas students. More surprising and rather worrying, now that Frank Paish had been made a full Professor of Finance with extra duties, he wished to give up being the Assistant Editor of *Economica* and had to be replaced. I was asked by its Managing Editors, Professors Hayek and Roy Allen, to succeed him. Why? I had unwittingly shown my hand as knowing something of continental economic thought, particularly German and Austrian contributions, and written a longish review of the first volume of ORDO, a series of essays by prominent German liberals who were to become influential in the German economic revival, if then largely unknown except to those of their number who were refugees in the UK or the USA. The review gave the impression of knowledge and experience well beyond my years and was absurdly pretentious, but Hayek approved of it.

This challenge of being tested so early in my career was too tempting to resist, and competed with the wish to find some outlet for my interest in being involved in discussion on policy matters. At least, entering the ranks of the Liberal Party as a foot soldier with the canvassers and support workers in the local branch, became a less attractive way of working my passage, even although it would be useful experience gained from being part of the rough and tumble of practical politics. My mind was made up by an unexpected consequence of my temporary 'fame'.

Before explaining what happened, it should be mentioned that I had written two further articles, one of which was an unusual commission to write about the finance of the welfare state for *The Round Table*, a journal devoted to Commonwealth affairs. This was passed over to me by Ronnie Tress, Reader in Public Finance at LSE, who was their first choice. He bolstered my confidence by approving of its contents, though puzzled, as was the journal editor, by what he thought was an Anglo-Saxon expression in it—'outwith'. This betrayed my origins, for it is a fine Scots word sanctioned by use in legal documents, the equivalent of standard English being 'outside'. I lost the battle to leave it in. Also all articles in this journal were unsigned. I did not have the temerity to question this, but a well-informed colleague explained that this was common practice with journals and periodicals and was supposedly an indication of their fine quality and recognised prestige! Who was I to question this, being content to have been paid what to me seemed a generous sum.

The second attempt to build on a growing interest in the broader questions of social policy was an examination of some of the alternatives to the National Insurance system which recommended the amalgamation of the British tax and transfer system as the logical result of the perceived necessity to finance the social security system out of general revenue to relieve the burden of compulsory insurance against unemployment, old age and disability which might otherwise be intolerable to working people. Its examination grew naturally out of my *Economica* article, and I thought it would make a useful contribution to the contemporary debate. I sent it to *The Political Quarterly*, the joint editors being Leonard Woolf and William Robson (Professor of Public Administration at LSE). This proved to be a mistake. Robson rang me up and berated me for sending what appeared to be 'a piece of liberal propaganda' which a good solid Socialist periodical could not possibly publish. It was in vain that I argued that James Meade, who had given this negative tax proposal a run for its money in his recent writings, was a member of the Labour Party. The 'piece of propaganda' was firmly rejected and remained unpublished, never to see the light of day. (I must add that when I knew 'Willie' better, he turned out to be one of the most charming of senior colleagues, though he had his sensitivities on political questions.)

However, my attempts to interest a wider range of disciplines in the economics of social policy did not go unrewarded. Two years after Willie's rejection of my piece and my associated dejection, I was approached by Richard Titmuss, newly appointed as Professor of Social Administration, about my views on the reform of national insurance . Curiously enough, it was not my criticisms of the administrative aspects of the new National Insurance system which interested him but those relating to the distribution of income. He was sufficiently impressed with the idea of tying together national insurance with generalized income support to mention my work in his inaugural lecture. Indeed, not long after that he encouraged me to apply for the newly created post of Reader in Social Policy which came up much at the same time as the vacant Readership in Public Finance (see Chapter 5 below). However, the temptation of early promotion to an impecunious lecturer was outweighed by a growing commitment to improving my skills as an economist and to the seeking of 'liberal' solutions to distributional problems. Richard has been described as 'the

standard bearer of the welfare state', a fitting description
and a clear indication of his growing rejection of 'market'
solutions to welfare problems and his later pervasive influence on socialist thinking coupled with his active part in
seeking to have his proposals adopted. Although I could
never come to agree with him on policy matters, I remember
with gratitude his kindness to me when I was one of his
junior colleagues.[1]

### IV: Opportunity Knocks

In the autumn of 1949 I had a visit from Margot Naylor, then
an established financial journalist and, like her husband,
Guy, a staunch Liberal. She had agreed to help Guy who
had been appointed Chairman of a Liberal Party Committee
on The Reform of Income Tax and Social Security Payments,
by acting as Minute Secretary. She explained that the setting
up of this Committee was largely on the initiative of the
Women's Federation of the Liberal Party who were very
impressed with the pioneering work of Lady Rhys Williams,
then still a Liberal activist of enormous energy and, in the
best sense, 'pushfulness'. That formidable lady had already
published a pamphlet *Something to Look Forward To* (1943)
offering an alternative approach to the Beveridge Plan. Its
influence with the Liberal ladies must have been something
of an embarrassment to the Liberal Executive because
Beveridge, as a newly-created peer, sat on the Liberal
benches and had enormous prestige as the designer of a
now internationally influential reform of social security.
Undeterred, the Liberal ladies pressed for an examination
of the Rhys Williams plan, and were asked to nominate
membership of the proposed Committee. Not unnaturally,

---

[1]    Liberally minded economists were to display considerable
differences in their view as to how they should take account of
Titmuss's strictures on economic analysis in the formulation of social
policy. However, that he became to be given serious attention is
demonstrated in his meriting an entry in the standard British
encyclopedia on Economics [see the article by Murray Milgate, on
'Titmuss, Richard Morris (1907–1973)', *The New Palgrave Dictionary of
Economics* (eds. Eatwell, Milgate and Newman ) Volume 4 , 1987,
pp. 655–656].

they suggested the names of some prominent members of their own ranks, including my colleague, Nancy Seear, Lecturer in Personnel Management at LSE, and whose students attended my introductory course on Economics. But the Women's Federation saw the need for some economics input and asked Frank Paish to be a member, and I suppose he and Nancy suggested my name as someone who would help Frank with the donkey work of statistical calculation. Frank recommended that I be a member as he preferred not to serve. Hence Margot's visit to look me over to confirm my competence and my degree of commitment to liberalism. Being an experienced member of the Civil Service Commission, she knew what questions to ask me. I must have passed muster and later she and Guy became friends of Margaret and myself, only cut short by Margot's tragic early death at the height of her career.

The preparation of *The Reform of Income Tax and Social Security Payments* provided a tyro with an object lesson in organisational skill which I have never forgotten. First of all, the Chairman, Guy Naylor, took stock of our availability for attendance at meetings, the time we might be able to spare for these and for 'home work', and the spread of expertise and experience among us. It was clear that long discussion of procedure and content of the report in advance of the hard work of preparation, the besetting sin of professional committees, was to be avoided, and in any case was constrained by the busy schedules of the participants. Nevertheless, the fact that there are many calls on their time is very often an indication of their suitability as members. The Chairman rightly concluded that a large number of formal meetings would be both impossible to arrange and not the most effective way of employing our skills. As the Report states (p. 5): 'much of our most useful work was bound to consist of individual study and investigation, the results of which were contributed to our common discussion'.

The second principle of operation was to be clear about the aims of the Report and its implications for the time and effort to achieve them, the invoking of this principle requiring us to be quite clear what to *exclude* from consideration and the justification for doing so.

With a general idea of the time resources and our aims, the Chairman must have some 'critical path' in mind which delineates who does what and when. This certainly did mean getting round the table to seek agreement that we would undertake assigned tasks presupposing that there was general agreement about the relative priority given to different issues, who was in the lead on examining them and with a definite time scale agreed. A good Chairman, as Guy turned out to be, needs to exert his authority in order to have a succession of drafts prepared and, if possible, circulated in advance of joint meetings, so that the meetings themselves are working sessions and not turned into talking shops. One useful way of reinforcing 'discipline' is by the Chairman setting a good example, often by taking on the study of one important general issue and by keeping an eye on complementary or rival work in the same field of enquiry and 'bombarding' members with cuttings from a selected range of periodicals and the press. It is not enough to take responsibility for the preparation of the agenda, to determine when and where a meeting is to be held, and to see that any necessary documents are circulated in advance or available at any meeting.

A final requirement is for the provision of members with a clear idea for whom the Report is written, which may range from a confidential report to a client, to a Report designed for the widest public discussion. This must affect the content, the style and the technical level of the final document. Again, an active Chairman can set an example and if lucky may be able to appoint an experienced Minute Secretary with drafting skills to 'fill out' the Chairman's thoughts. Such an aide can be invaluable if technical input, such as economic analysis, must be translated into intelligible prose and which its perpetrator can agree to.

Guy Naylor, as Chairman, could call upon only very limited Party resources although we were extremely fortunate that his own commitment to liberalism was shared by Margot, acting as Minute Secretary. Communication was by 'snail mail', although that was the acme of efficiency compared with today, and by an unreliable and relatively expensive telephone service — no email in those days. Some members might have been able to type, usually with two fingers, but several sent in their drafts in longhand. Copying papers was a very slow process compared with downloading today.

Despite these difficulties, but with some hard pounding, Guy was able to hand the Report to the printer, well before it had to run the gauntlet of Liberal Party committees, and the annual Assembly scheduled for the autumn of 1950 where it was hoped it would be recommended for general approval. I expected that at least I would discover how to find my way round the government reports and learn something about the machinery of decision making in politics, without becoming an apologist for policies that I did not believe in and bearing in mind the more urgent necessity of improving my skills as a professional economist. If this scenario had been correct, there would be little further to be said. But the subsequent history of the Report, or rather the ideas it contained, were to determine otherwise, opening up a debate on the economics of the welfare state that has lasted until the present day. Why that was so requires me to set out its analysis and findings in some detail.

**Annex 4.1:　Extract from *The National Insurance Funds*,
Alan T. Peacock, pp. 238–39
(reprinted from *Economica*, August 1949)**

In the past the special problems of unemployment insurance justified a separate budgetary policy. But in the case of a National Insurance scheme, which, financially considered, is a social service, do the uses of the Funds described above really indicate that the continuance of separate National Insurance accounting quite outside the framework of Government finance is at all necessary? Would it not be simpler and more sensible to make Treasury control more explicit and to integrate the National Insurance accounts with the Revenue and Capital Accounts of the public sector? Apart from the simplification this would produce in the complicated system of Government accounting it would get rid of the elaborate ritual of transferring balances from the Exchequer to the Funds and back again in order to keep up the pretence that the scheme is based on insurance principles. Furthermore, it is quite possible that, as in the Unemployment Fund, the Reserve Fund might be a source of considerable embarrassment to the Government if, as the funds accumulated, representatives of the main contributors such as employers' organisations and trade unions began to demand reductions in contributions and increased benefits[2] which might not be warranted by the current financial situation.

　Political considerations may invalidate this suggestion and some semblance of independence may thus be important. Socially considered, whatever method of financing the scheme is employed the acceptance of the principle of collective risk, particularly with regard to unemployment, necessitates the preservation of the vital distinction between unemployment insurance and unemployment assistance, between the payment of benefit as a right and the payment of benefit as an act of charity. But even from the

---

[2]　In the House of Commons on the 27th April, 1948, the Minister of National Insurance was urged to raise unemployment benefit in view of the growth in the accumulated funds. See *Parliamentary Debates* (H of C), Vol. 450, 1947–48

economic point of view it may be wise to retain the present system of separate accounting.

# Chapter 5

# Joining the Firing Line

## I: Down to Work

The main task of the Committee was to consider the problem of squaring the perceived need for increasing taxation
to pay for social security with maintaining the incentives to
work and save, without undermining the freedom of individual citizens to make their own economic decisions. It
called for a good deal more than the kind of musings of my
own associated with pondering the war-time writings of
Beveridge and Hayek, pinpointed in the crying out for some
empirical foundation to support any logical scheme. While
this requirement was to become very much my concern as a
member of the committee, there was a more practical difficulty which was how to present some rather novel ideas to
longstanding members of the Liberal Party Executive, more
immediately worried about the declining fortunes of the
Party itself. It would seem to them that the Party would gain
most in the way of public exposure, recognition and possible votes by nailing their colours to the Beveridgean mast,
given the high reputation of Beveridge himself and his
active campaigning for the Party, eventually leading, after
he ceased to be an MP, to his becoming a Peer and opting to
sit in the Liberal benches, as John Maynard Keynes had
done.

Fortunately, there had been an important precedent for
considering an approach to our problem associated with the
Party, and with a particular appeal to the active women

members of the Executive who had been so impressed with the political writings of one of their number—Lady Juliet Rhys Williams. She had sought an answer to an important difficulty presented by a social security scheme built round the relief of poverty, where it was quite generally accepted that providing such relief could undermine the incentive to seek employment. Her answer was what today is known as a negative income tax approach. With the wartime extension of the income tax system, it seemed possible to bring all the working population and their families into the tax 'net' with an exemption for the lowest income bands. However, while this revealed a simple way of correcting income inequalities, two adjustments would need to be made. Income correction could not be guaranteed by the system if a considerable proportion of the working population had incomes below the exemption limit for income tax relief. The first adjustment could be made by a system of negative taxation, by which those below the exemption limit would be entitled to some positive payment. The second adjustment arose from the necessity of recognising that positive payments were already being made on a selective basis in the form of unemployment, sickness benefits and benefits in kind, such as rent rebates in local authority housing and food subsidies. A negative income tax system offered an opportunity to simplify the system by providing all taxpayers with a positive allowance, whether or not they were in work, which, it was claimed, would create an enormous simplification in the highly complicated system of national insurance already in the process of development. This could be done by providing the positive allowances tax free and raising income tax from a single rate on all incomes above this limit, making it possible to abolish the complicated exemption provisions necessary in taking account of individual family circumstances.

   This is a rough summary of the Committee's approach to their task, paying tribute on the way to Lady Rhys Williams, but still concerned about one principal matter. The distributional problem, if not solved, was more nearly so by the integration of money payments with the tax system. This depended on the incidence of the entire tax structure and also on the content and the size of the negative tax payments and how far these offset the tax burdens throughout the income distribution. One had to be able to demonstrate what the orders of magnitude applied by these proposals would tell us before knowing what the effects of the scheme would be. The Committee then turned towards Frank Paish and myself, leaving me to burrow away as fast as I could to conjure up the necessary data. Only then could one appraise the central innovation in the scheme, namely that the positive payments would be paid, taking account of family size, whether or not the household wage earners were employed. It seemed reasonable to suppose that the incentive to work would then depend on the relation between the size of the positive payments and the difference between it and the alternative opportunities to enter the labour force or to remain in work, account being taken of the value attached to leisure in both choices, if choice there was.

Could such a scheme really work? The answer to this question, as mentioned above, depended on the calculations I had to undertake in order to demonstrate how total tax revenue would be altered by the need to finance some 'acceptable' minimum income level. This turned out to be a more extensive task than I had bargained for.

It was comparatively easy to draw up a table showing how the pre- and post-distribution of income would be affected by alternative models embodying alternative concepts of a minimum income and given rates of income tax. However, any scheme had to take a more comprehensive indication of the principles behind it and the constraints on fulfilling them by this new element in the highly sophisticated and complicated UK fiscal system. This would mean offering calculations that were more than merely illustrative, but were derived from proposed adjustment in the actual system, especially if the scheme was designed to influence public opinion generally and political debate in particular. Somehow, once regarded as a necessary evil, public discussions and Parliamentary debates in particular now fed greedily on the growing deluge of official statistics that were becoming available from the Central Office and Inland Revenue.

Consider now the conditions that would have to be met in a 'workable' scheme:

i.    The principle involved required the identification of a measurable minimum income level. A good deal of research had gone into the preparation of 'human needs' diets and in obtaining some consensus on what constituted escape from the 'poverty trap', but a definition of minimum income was bound to be subjective and therefore open to political debate. The committee took an entirely pragmatic view and did not attempt to justify any particular figure, but emphasised that the upper limit to a minimum level was constrained by the limitations on its finance which in turn would depend on the productive power of the nation and how this might be affected by any disincentives a negative income tax scheme might produce. The crucial element in the definition was that poverty was to be defined in abso-lute terms, so that the minimum income level remained fixed in real terms (ie after allowing for changes in the cost of living) and was unrelated to the 'real' growth in the econ-omy. The idea that the 'poverty line' should shift upwards as average real incomes grew is of later origin. By the 1970s, minimum income was sometimes defined as 25 per cent of average income, but this is disputed as being too niggardly. Clearly, this change is indicative of continuing disagree-ment about the 'ideal' income distribution. It is mentioned because the impetus given to this debate is closely associ-ated with the definition of poverty and how far relief of pov-erty alone is the cardinal element in defining and achieving some optimal income distribution. For many political phi-losophers seeking to influence official policy, removing the poverty trap did not go far enough.

ii. The scheme would lack credence if it could not be demonstrated that it took a responsible view of its cost to the public. This might have been a rather old-fashioned view alongside the common assumption that, after WW2, the British economy would suffer from lack of effective demand with productive resources, notably labour, under-employed. If a scheme of this sort were to require deficit spending, then this would be no barrier to its introduction. Keynes had already rejected this crude interpretation of his so-called 'depression economics', but had died in 1946 without sufficiently clarifying his position, while distinguished disciples, such as James Meade and Roy Harrod, had already shown how the Keynesian engine should go in reverse in a situation of overfull employment. Meade, in commending the Rhys Williams scheme, had claimed that it could be operated as a contra-cyclical device if under-employment re-emerged. The Committee quite readily accepted that any changes required by their scheme had to be 'fiscal-neutral', requiring that the overall burden of taxation must not be increased.

iii. A clear indication was necessary as to the coverage of the scheme. The Committee laid great stress on keeping before us a liberal concept of the meaning and purpose of state-supplied benefits. To quote para 31 of the Report which I had a hand in drafting — hence its rather youthful and schoolmasterish tone —

> we are not much attracted by the paternalistic system, whether the role of father is assumed by conservatives or socialists ... people learn to behave as adults only if they are allowed to make their own mistakes and as far as possible spend their own money ... this means that we prefer the individual to spend his earnings as he sees fit, and that where an individual's spending power depends upon a subsidy in cash and not in kind.

The hold that this principle had on me lasts until this day and governed much of the ideas on liberal economic and social policy that I was later allowed to present in Liberal Party circles, but eventually led to my 'downfall'. But the immediate problem was not that of reaching whole-hearted agreement to the principle but the extent to which it would determine the scope of our reforms. One has to remember that there had been a major increase in subsidies in kind, partly as wartime measures when rationing was imperative and its 'fairness' depending on targeting vulnerable groups, and partly in line with Labour philosophy and politics, notably in the provision of local government housing at highly subsidised rents. (What would today be regarded as a particularly bizarre form of subsidy was one which reduced the price of tobacco for pensioners, which was not abolished until 1955!) It would not be feasible to propose scrapping these on a large scale without encountering the usual 'excuse' of it not being feasible to do so.

Our response to the first problem was conditioned by the constraint indicated by the second. Examination of the Rhys Williams data raised two doubts. She offered what appeared at the time to be generous positive payments, as compared to the existing ones payable to the unemployed, sick and pensioners. It was conceivable that alone these would perhaps blunt the incentive to work (see *The Reform of Income Tax and Social Security (RITSS)*, paras 43–51), particularly when her calculations of the compensating amount of revenue to be raised from a proportional income tax, in accordance with the desire to simplify its collection, would require a rate of 6s/8d in the pound (or 33%). We were ourselves to discover that this would not cover the amount of revenue loss and Lady Rhys Williams proposed that the difference could be met by what amounted to a poll-tax — a similar proposal being made by James Meade (op. cit.). A disincentive effect seemed readily to be assumed if this meant that the effect of entering the lowest tax bracket would be to reduce any extra income by a third. (A great deal of ink has since been used up by economists indulged in testing whether this assumption stands up to both analytical respectability and empirical verification!)

Paul Chambers (see *RITSS*, paras 59–61), ex-senior official of the Inland Revenue and later to become Chairman of ICI, saw the solution in a ruthless cutting in the spread of allowances, which should only be paid in respect of dependants, in order to bring down the standard rate of income tax to 3/- in the pound, or 15%, but still requiring additional tax on incomes above £500 pa. Therefore, both the simplicity of the tax system would be modified and the limited range and amount of allowances would be well below those that would make it worthwhile considering it as an income support scheme.

We decided (see *RITSS*, para 62) that the 'best practicable reform (would) lie somewhere between the generosity of Lady Rhys Williams and the parsimony of Mr Chambers', it being agreed amongst us that there appeared to be no completely successful way of providing both absolute social security and the maximising of incentive. We started, as it were, at the 'Chambers' end' of the debate, and fixed the proportional rate of income tax at 5/- in the pound, or 25%, and I was left to calculate the associated revenue yield. That was not an easy thing to do. It was not simply a question of obtaining data on aggregate personal incomes, for a considerable proportion of income tax was raised from income accruing abroad but liable to UK tax and one had to consider whether or not to include business undistributed profits in the tax base. There was the more awkward problem as to whether the yield of incomes itself would be affected by the change in the tax system that we were proposing, and how long it would take before such a change would be reflected in the revenue yield. It seemed better to show awareness of the difficulty, and, like the Presbyterian Scots preacher faced with a knotty theological problem in his sermon, to look it squarely in the face — and pass it by. At least, we showed where we started from — how revenue yield would look if we took the latest figures of total personal incomes and its distribution by income group — data now available and published by the Inland Revenue — and substitute our scheme for the existing system, no change assumed in the pre-tax distribution of personal income. However, even this calculation did not end the process of statistical illustration, because it transpired that our assumed 'maximum' proportional tax rate would not be sufficient to cover the cost of our assumed negative tax provisions which were to be somewhat more generous than those of Chambers but less generous than those of Rhys Williams.

In some ways it was as well that we were left with a balance of revenue to meet, because a change to comprehensive proportionality would have resulted in an increase in the inequality of incomes after tax, compared to the existing progressive tax regime. This highlighted another aspect of the incentive issue, namely the effects of tax changes on incentives at different income levels and different ways of earning income subject to different degrees of risk. Again, this matter was left on one side, because we felt obliged to assume that a scheme which increased income inequality, though it could be made compatible with a negative income system, would be highly unpopular. This was the principal reason for being sceptical of meeting any revenue deficiency by using a poll tax, as suggested by both James Meade and Lady Rhys Williams, unless, of course, some other changes could be made simultaneously in the fiscal system. So we felt it necessary to raise the extra revenue by a supplementary tax of 2s and 3s respectively on the excess of earned and unearned income above £600 a year with the 3s rate also applied to undistributed profits. Such a proposal reduced the possibility of simplifying the tax system and would require personal assessments for higher income receivers.

## II: Reactions

The Report went to the printer in March 1950 and was published the following month as *The Reform of Income and Social Security Payments*. A potted history of what followed would read as follows:

- April and May 1950, press presentation and comment and ensuing correspondence;
- Summer 1950, discussion by Liberal Party Executive and endorsement at Liberal Party Conference in September 1950;
- Late 1950, Announcement of a Royal Commission on Taxation of Profits and Income;

- Spring 1951, preparation of evidence to the commission from Liberal Party and separately by Lady Rhys Williams;

- Spring 1951, Commission referred both Liberal Party and Rhys Williams schemes to Inland Revenue alongside consideration of other schemes for comment;

- July 1951, Oral Evidence by the Inland Revenue, Lady Rhys Williams and Liberal Party to the Commission;

- 1955/1957, Commission publish their views as separate report in advance of their main Report.

Here I was, only three years into my academic career and thrown into the deep end of public discussion. I could hardly refuse to take part in the progression of events, though worried about where it fitted in to my commitments to my job, and whether I was able to face exposure to public criticism, not having expected to be anywhere near a position where anyone would take a blind bit of notice of my efforts. A narrative of the succession of events in which I became involved is much less important than an account of what I believe anyone in my position would have learnt from the experience.

A first addition to my knowledge was the appearance of the press reports. At the time this event seemed important to me. The world would hear about the report, ponder its contents and would be changed. Of course, nothing changed. I was surprised to see a very short account of its contents in the *Manchester Guardian*, to give that paper's original title. Half a column was all it got, most of it in small print (*Manchester Guardian*, 26 April 1950). It was about the same length as the next column entry reporting a debate on bread making in the House of Lords in which Lord Sempill spoke with some authority, it being revealed that he baked his own bread. I was too quick in my reaction of disappointment, fuelled by the fact that the (then) much more cautious *The Times* had the same day published a leader on our proposals. I had also failed to spot a leader in the *Manchester Guardian* advocating speed in preparing our proposals for the Liberal Party autumn conference, so as to be ready for the next election.

Somehow I had expected more, but it was a wise elderly colleague at LSE who, some years later when I had published my first book on *The Economics of National Insurance (1952)*, wished me well:

> Alan, you will regard your literary first-born as a gift to the world, as I did many years ago, but if you step outside you will see that somehow the event goes unremarked. We learn the simple economic truth that broadsheets measure the attention given to your public utterances by the alternatives they forego, as measured by what they think their readers (and advertisers) will prefer.

Their supply of alternatives may nowadays change with extraordinary rapidity, calling for last-minute decisions taking account of the crowding out of earlier news by the latest sensations. Nor must one assume that those obliged to reveal to the world what they are doing, in politics, often determined by statutory requirements covering what the public claim to have the right to know, always want to publish such information. We have become increasingly confronted by this subtle interplay of what the press wants and demands and how its control is supplied by governments and influential non-governmental organisations (NGOs) using such dodges as reporting items unfavourable to themselves in a form which is unlikely to receive attention. Going back to 1950, one realises that we had been fortunate to be taken seriously and to have had a reasonable reception.

Education about the ways of the Press did not end there. On their side, interest in the scheme and the influence of Lady Rhys Williams on the general idea of amalgamation of income tax and social security remained in being and was spasmodically referred to. There was an immediate response to publication from a prominent Tory, using the attractive weapon of combining virulent criticism of all aspects of the scheme with icy politeness (see Geoffrey Bracken, *Manchester Guardian*, 17 May 1950) and I was fielded to reply in what was my very first letter in the national press, unless one counted a jejeune effort in *The Scotsman* when, as an undergraduate in 1947, I corrected a wrong impression of the origin of Mendelssohn's inspiration for his Hebridean Overture by quoting *Grove's Dictionary*! (Malcolm Knox, my Professor, was most impressed, being himself very interested in music, so it did me no harm!) But this was a serious matter because Bracken had questioned the statistical estimates for which I had been made responsible.

What happened was instructive. I considered how to reply and wrote a measured defence of our calculations (see *Manchester Guardian*, 26 May 1950), but Lady Rhys Williams upstaged me with an immediate response (*Manchester Guardian*, 22 May 1950) which was both a reply to Bracken's broad canvas of generalities and a close-knit exposition of her whole approach. It was, however, a useful prelude to my own reply because she defended our calculations which she flatteringly ascribed to 'a specialist in the area' and were to be treated as 'careful estimates', and not as 'casual statements'. So the second lesson to be learnt is that with the Press, strike while the iron is hot, remembering how hot their 'iron' always has to be! It was more difficult in those days to publish letters in *The Times*, and I have known colleagues sufficiently impressed with achieving their acceptance to record the fact in their professional list of published work! (Several years later, when I used to appear on the Liberal platform offering candidates support, I had a hilarious discussion on the difficulties of entry into *The Times* correspondence column with William Douglas-Home, the playwright, who had stood as a candidate for South Edinburgh in the 1962 election. He claimed a high strike rate in reaching these dizzy heights, which he attributed to having his letters delivered by hand to Printing House Square by a lady wearing gloves (employed by that well known and prestigious agency, Universal Aunts)!

There was now a welcome breathing space in the public debate until *The Economist* reported its reactions to the setting up of a Royal Commission to enquire into the operation of the taxation of profits and income (see *The Economist*, 5 August 1950). It paid particular attention to the examination of Lady Rhys Williams' scheme, and the necessity to include it and 'possible variants' in the Commission's Terms of Reference, adding that 'it has many attractions and presents as many difficulties'. Our Chairman now entered the lists, and wrote a spirited letter (*The Economist*, 17 August 1950) chiding *The Economist* for not having reviewed our own consideration of the 'many difficulties' which at least we had faced up to. It was an integral part of our attempt to gain wider consideration of how a Liberal approach to policy matters far transcends its lack of representation in the process of government. This was all the more reason for regretting that he felt unable to continue to take an active part in the attempt to obtain a hearing, though, when it came to appearing in front of the Royal Commission in the following year, we had welcome support from one of the *grands seigneurs* of the Party, Sir Arthur Comyns Carr, Vice President and later President.

The last phase of the initial reception of the report culminated in the fulfilment of our main expectation, namely that the annual Party Conference in September would see its adoption as Liberal policy. This was in fact achieved by the skilful presentation of an integrated list of economics measures, notable for their welcome consistency with the principles of Liberalism. Our scheme fitted in to the requirement of increasing the responsibility of the individual household for its allocation of its income, and that of government through greater efficiency in public spending, bearing in mind the commitment to maintain an adequate social security system, and defence provision. The underlying need to improve productive efficiency which would make it possible to realise our aims required government measures to promote competition and freedom in international trade and, more controversially perhaps, in giving particular attention to policies encouraging industrial co-ownership. This does not tell us very much about how a Liberal administration might have shaped up to implementing such policies. But 'principles must precede policies' is a good Liberal principle in itself and all credit must be given to Frank Byers, the then active President of the Liberal Executive, for his robust presentation of our economics agenda.

**Annex 5.1: Extract from *Reform of Income Tax and Social Security Payments*, pp. 6–8, paras 10–17**

10. It would be very dangerous to examine questions of taxation or of 'social security'[1] in isolation and without relating them to the general economic position of the community affected. Neither taxation nor 'social security' create wealth; they merely redistribute it, the one by taking it away, and the other by returning it in different shares. It is obvious that the problem of the redistribution of wealth is only secondary to the problem of creating it and to the question of how much exists to be redistributed.

11. In a primitive community the standard of life of each member is so low that there is no margin for redistribution: if anything is taken from one citizen and given to another it will either impoverish the one from whom it is taken or be insufficient to benefit the one to whom it is given. It is only a relatively prosperous community that can support substantial systems of taxation and subsidisation; but however prosperous it may be the production of the wealth must be the primary consideration.

12. Even in the case of a prosperous community there must evidently be a proper proportion between the amount taken in taxation and the total amount of the wealth. This proportion is a vital consideration in relation both to the question of 'incentive' and to the question of the pattern of society which it is desired to achieve.

13. [We deal more fully below with the question of incentive, and] it will be sufficient here merely to point out the obvious fact that if too great a proportion is taken away in taxation it may destroy the incentive to earn the little that is left, and that if too much is distributed in subsidies it may destroy the incentive of the individual to make sufficient effort on his own behalf. In both cases the production of wealth will be lowered, the total out of which taxation can be raised and out of which subsidies can be paid will

---

[1] We use this expression to describe state systems for augmenting personal or family consuming power.

become insufficient, and the whole system will be in jeopardy.

14. It is equally obvious that the pattern of society is considerably affected by the proportion which taxation and subsidy bears to the national income. Theoretically the whole wealth of the community could be collected into the hands of the Government and then redistributed in a way that would be both fairer and more efficient than has been achieved under any other system. Quite apart, however, from whether any consequent loss of incentive would make this system impossible in practice, it is evident that the pattern of society would be very different, and that there must at least be some loss of personal freedom, personal choice and personal responsibility. Whatever views may be held of the merits of the 'welfare state' it cannot be denied that these dangers are implicit in it, and its advantages must be weighed against them so that it is not pushed beyond the point where they are outweighed by the disadvantages, with their attendant evil effects upon the liberty, humanity and moral fibre of the people.

15. Furthermore, even in the case of a prosperous community where the proportion has been satisfactorily assessed in relation both to the retention of incentive and the preservation of a reasonably free society, there is a further consideration to be borne in mind: is the proportion which is taken in tax being satisfactorily used, and are any subsidies which are granted being distributed to the best advantage? Although the amount of taxation may not be excessive from the standpoints of freedom and incentive, the manner in which it is employed or the system by which it is levied may diminish the total real wealth of the community or may prove unnecessarily disincentive in its operation.

16. It is clear that even a low degree of taxation and subsidisation might have this effect. If, for example, the Government were to devote the resources raised by taxation to the building of grandiose public monuments or temporary spectacles when the people would have preferred houses, the community would lose real wealth not merely

from the point of view of the individuals who had been taxed but absolutely as a community. If the Government devote such resources to, for example, an ill-considered scheme of colonial development, the community is similarly worse off in an absolute sense than if those resources had remained in private hands and had been more fruitfully employed. If subsidies are given to the wrong persons (for example, to the well-to-do and not those who need them) or for a wrong purpose (for example, to encourage monopoly or to bolster up incompetence) there is equally an absolute loss to the community. One method of raising tax may likewise be more impoverishing than another which shows the same yield — as, for example, where the rate of tax rises abruptly and at the wrong income levels from the point of view of incentive, or where the incidence of taxation is such as to encourage stagnation rather than enterprise and adventure.

17. All these basic factors to which we have called attention may (and often do) exist together at the same time and interact upon one another. No proposals in the field of reformed taxation or 'social security' can be sound or honest which do not recognise that any measure which will produce an advantage in one direction is almost certain to produce at least some disadvantage in another, and that any solution can at best be no more than a compromise between the different advantages which have a claim to consideration and the various disadvantages which must inevitably accompany the adoption of any solution at all.

Chapter 6

# The Fire is Returned

## I: Royal Commission on the Taxation of Profits and Income

It was reasonable to suppose that our Report would have some influence on the direction of Liberal policy and one hoped against hope that it would be taken out and dusted down at some time in the future—looking very distant in 1950—and embodied in a major act of reform by some future Liberal Government. One could then concentrate on some of the wider questions raised about the principles of a Liberal social policy which took account of the realities of the UK's economic progress and prospects. While this is what happened in my own case, I had not expected that the prospect of thinking deep thoughts in true academic fashion would need to be harnessed to an urgent call to help from the Party to prepare and submit written evidence and face oral examination by a Royal Commission on the Taxation of Profits and Income (henceforth the RCTPI) appointed the following year, 1951. This was because the Terms of Reference of the Commission covered general social and economic questions arising from the impact of the direct tax system. Apart from the analysis of the economic effects of the present system and how tax structure might be improved to meet the demands of economic and social policy, the Commission was specifically asked to consider the question: 'Would it be advantageous to link Income Tax with social security payments and contributions?' We would be expected to provide evidence within three months, so that the first task of those of us invited by the Party to give evidence was to consider if any revisions were needed in our analysis and conclusions.

Royal Commissions, consisting of the great and the good advising governments on matters of importance, are no longer a prime source of revelation to the public on the conduct of affairs of government and how they might be improved. The tendency nowadays is for Secretaries of State to surround themselves with or summon specialist advisers for such purposes, often, it must be regretted, to show that they are both busy and important in promoting the public weal. The demand for these services, still occasionally met by *ad hoc* Committees of Enquiry instead of bodies with a regal title, varies with the concerns of the government in power. It can be a response to demand to deal particularly with some long-term problem such as public concern at an ageing and slow-growing population, represented by the Royal Commission on Population which had led to the introduction of Family Allowances after WW2. It can be a way for a government to play for time, as with Harold Wilson's worries about the unwelcome appearance of Welsh Nationalists elected to the House of Commons in 1964, which led to the appointment of the Royal Commission on the Constitution in the late 1960s, of which I became a member (with the grand title of Commissioner). In the case of the RCTPI, it was the increasing pressures put on the direct tax system by the major reforms introduced by the Labour Government, such as the extension of the social security system, the provision of health which involved increasing the size of government expenditure relative to national income, our obligations to pay off foreign lending and the unexpected continuance of a high level of public expenditure on defence.

The supply of expertise that a Royal Commission might command would depend on how the government and its advisers viewed the problems it had to deal with. It was customary to appoint a prominent lawyer, a High Court judge for instance, as Chairman, and in the case of economic questions, add in a prominent accountant together with a representative of business and of the trades unions, and even a Professor of Economics or Fellow usually recruited from one of the 'two universities', though in the case of the Royal Commission on Population it had been decided to take the radical step of including an Edinburgh Professor (though one with civil service experience) in the form of Sir Alexander Gray. In the case of RCTPI, the traditional pattern was followed, but history was made by including two formidable economists as members, Nicholas Kaldor from Cambridge and John Hicks from Oxford. My colleagues and I at the LSE were clearly aware of this change, but I little thought that I would one day have to take a rather more close interest in their activities.

## II: The 'Revenue' Get Busy

The Commission, through its Chairman, was bound to consider and to press for help, not only to cope with the obvious administrative tasks required of it, but also, particularly in the case of their remit, to produce analysis and commentary on written submissions, and, where appropriate, account of what their own experience and expertise had to offer by way of advice. I know from later experience that negotiation of demands for such resources is a difficult art. One requires skilled manpower and possibly the services of outside consultants, not to speak of seeking assurance that Commissioners, who would give their services free, would not be out of pocket from having to spend a good deal of their time on Commission business. However, particular features of the RCTPI's work required not only access to the statistical resources of government and notably that of the Inland Revenue, but also drawing on the experience of the Inland Revenue itself with its long history of advice to successive governments on the problems of revenue raising. Clearly, the Inland Revenue would be in the lead on advice-giving, and would have the added incentive of wishing to influence the Commission's work, as its own interests in how the tax system should be run would be bound to be affected by the RCTPI's conclusions.

The situation developed as one might have expected, and the Inland Revenue started the process of advice-giving by pitching in on the reforms suggested by ourselves, taking account of the pioneering efforts of Lady Rhys Williams and the strong professional backing received by her from *The Economist* at various times and James Meade. Indeed, the RCTPI had hardly had time to catch their breath when the Inland Revenue produced a memorandum, later published in full, attached to their oral evidence to the Commission. This formed the basis of the extensive questioning of Lady Rhys Williams and ourselves that the Commission threw in our direction when a team of us appeared before it in July 1951. The Inland Revenue evidence, as I shall try to make clear, was a hatchet job, and a very effective one at that. It was to prove difficult to question their calculations on the effects of our scheme on the distribution of income, because the source of our information, such as was made available, was the Inland Revenue itself, then having a monopoly, not even today eroded, of the tax and income data on which our calculations had to be based.

It is perhaps worth speculating on why the Inland Revenue appeared to be so concerned about our evidence, for it raises a general point about its position as a very important part of the government machine. First, it was a natural source of advice on the actual workings of the tax system, going back centuries, with a considered, if coloured, view of what was 'workable' in making changes in it. In that respect, it had an in-built suspicion of new, radical schemes which might entail major changes in its own way of doing things. This is not to say that the Inland Revenue was totally opposed to any form of innovation, and one notes that the famous PAYE scheme of deducting income tax at source, placing the responsibility in law for the collection and the burden of doing so on employers and introduced only a few years before 1951, ie during WW2, was an example of this kind. In short, any new development had to pass its tests for feasibility and become domesticated, if at all, only by adaptation to the Inland Revenue's principles of operation.

Second, the Inland Revenue did keep up with professional discussion by accountants, economists, lawyers and
political scientists of the principles of taxation, but in a
rather covert way. (I had two experiences of this later, once
when I referred a PhD student to the Inland Revenue who
wrote a decent thesis on the history of inheritance taxation
in the UK, and was supplied with some most interesting
memoranda on their views on the tax in relation to government policy, and later when they helped me work out the
quantitative effects on the possible introduction of an
annual wealth tax, where I was struck by their considerable
knowledge of the philosophy of wealth taxation.) But the
Inland Revenue's purpose was to be able to explain the
extent, that they usually regarded as negligible, to which
suggested reforms based on the principles of taxation were
practicable, and not because of some view on the desirability
of change itself. In the case of our scheme, which required
the amalgamation of social security and income taxation,
they were forced into the position of considering this
general issue because the Commission itself, and possibly
themselves, would be impressed that a former chief of the
Cabinet Economic Secretariat, James Meade, had given it
such a strong recommendation. The Inland Revenue would
be bound to be asked questions about it.

Third, there is a question left over from the above discussion as to what was the remit of the Inland Revenue
received from government, and the extent to which it was
influenced by the Inland Revenue itself. It can be encapsulated very briefly in the maxim 'protect the revenue', meaning that any scheme that reduced the yield of income tax,
and raised the costs of collection was to be opposed. Over
the years I have never subsequently come across any occasion when they qualified this interpretation of the maxim by
taking into account the possibility that a reduction in
income tax might be compensated by an increase in tax
yields in the rest of the economic system, eg through the
spending of any increase in income left after tax on goods
subject to Customs and Excise duties.

### III: The Tactics of Giving Evidence

Members of the Committee were called to give evidence to the RCTPI over two days in June and July 1951. The present author does not have the literary skill to do so, but it need only be said that the procedure, resembling appearance in Court, produces an atmosphere which might originally have been meant to remind witnesses of the solemnity of the occasion. Also the tendency even today to appoint High Court judges as Chair of Commissions induces witnesses with sufficient resources to employ counsel to handle the understandable tendency of inquisitors to set them traps. This was clearly in the minds of our own Chairman, who agreed to have Sir Arthur Comyns Carr QC take the lead.

It was a wise move, because what we expected to happen did happen. The Inland Revenue in their written evidence, after what must be admitted to be a useful summary of the various schemes, concentrated their fire on the Liberal memorandum. Fortunately, we were able to obtain a copy of the Inland Revenue evidence in advance of our appearance, so that Sir Arthur was well briefed on their line of attack. Leaving me to field questions about our calculations of the benefits and costs of our scheme, he was able to transform short, frank answers to specific questions into beautifully rounded statements of our philosophy of social welfare which were particularly critical of the Inland Revenue especially when they occasionally strayed into making what could only be personal judgements rather than technical criticisms. On my suggestion, he managed to persuade the Chairman, Lord Cohen, to agree to request that the Inland Revenue should offer us their help to revise our calculations so that they agreed with their own.

Sir Arthur's trenchant criticism of the Inland Revenue's tendency to torpedo the Liberal scheme by claiming that we had overestimated the benefits and underestimated costs made things easier for me in some ways, but more difficult in others. Firstly, the Inland Revenue, probably as a riposte, began, under instruction from Arthur Cockfield, only to answer specific queries from us about the disparities between their estimates and ours, whereas we had hoped that they would help us in such a way that we could arrive at least broad agreement between ourselves and the Inland Revenue. That put us at a clear disadvantage. Secondly, when it came to my turn to be put in the hot seat (see *Minutes of Evidence*, 18 July 1951), attention turned more towards the broader questions of the economic consequences of a radical change. It seemed only sensible to admit that no specific proof could be offered that a fully worked-out scheme resting on a firm statistical base, as we claimed it was, would produce a clear advantage in improving the incentives to work and save.

The terms of reference of the Commission precluded looking at the system of taxation and social security within the broader context of overall economic policy. Otherwise, it would have been possible to argue that there was no reason why the constraint of no change in revenue yields of income tax and National Insurance contributions should not be relaxed, offering forms of tax relief which were more likely to improve the incentive to work. If that required a deficit in our calculations, one could look for compensating changes in the tax system which made up the difference in other ways, always provided that poorer sections of the population suffered no offsetting increase in tax burdens. In an even broader context, government expenditure might be reduced in other directions, subject to the same constraints, bringing into prominence the further, important consideration that any final package must be based on the value judgements of the policy makers inevitably forced to trade off one set of policy objectives against another. But politicians get confused by this kind of economic logic and prefer to rely on simple maxims, such as 'protect the revenue', even if these can mislead them into taking bad decisions.

However, a Commission of *prominente*, average age twice my own, were unlikely to listen to a disquisition on the high theory of economic policy from a wet-behind-the-ears junior lecturer. I was brought onto more familiar ground when John Hicks and Nicky Kaldor asked a few technical questions about economic analysis. They were particularly interested in consequences of our proposed abolition of

National Insurance contributions paid by both employee and employer and the effect that would have on our calculations. I was far from sure how to reply and, although they did not make any comment to that effect, I considered that I had muffed it. I had assumed it was accepted by our Committee that the employer's contribution would now accrue as an addition to profits and therefore this would increase the yield of profits tax, and also that the reduction of the employee contribution would now increase the incomes of the earning population. In fact, what I should have emphasised is that *all* our calculations illustrated the 'first round' effects, where it was reasonable to assume that those responsible for paying taxes or receiving benefits were subject to the appropriate deductions from or additions to their income *other things being equal*. In the longer run, second and third round effects might be important. For example, the very idea that our scheme would encourage the incentive to work would depend on reactions to our proposed changes in the tax and social security regime itself.

The length of the proceedings precluded me from staying beyond this stage of this inquisition, which was unfortunate, because Sir Arthur and Nancy Seear in particular, were left to argue with one of the Commission members, W.F. Crick (a banker), who clearly believed that the new Beveridgean National Insurance scheme was sacrosanct. Indeed, this question has already arisen before, when Sir Arthur had to counter the suggestion that we would be rejecting the advice of one of Liberalism's most revered representatives conferred by a Labour government. His reply on that occasion was that our respect for Lord Beveridge could not be doubted but that this did not oblige us as fellow-Liberals to accept that there were no alternative ways of improving the social security system.

### IV: Aftermath

In the first years after the Commission questioned us, the scheme remained on the books as part of Liberal policy, along with other reforms, with the broad intention of trying to preserve, if not increase, the degree of individuals' control over their own resources, and to fuller participation in political decision making to promote Liberal views on how collective action should be undertaken but with safeguards against undue political interference. It joined such ideas as encouraging the growth of employee-managed firms — a long-standing liberal idea much favoured by John Stuart Mill a century before — and systems of proportional representation, again a favourite of John Stuart Mill, particularly appealing to patrician figures in the Party such as Violet Bonham Carter. (Several years later, on the one occasion when I was invited to a small discussion dinner party given by the Duke of Edinburgh, the subject being 'devolution', Lord Hailsham dismissed proportional representation by a typical aphorism: 'The trouble with proportional representation is that when you're out of power, you can't 'ave it, and when you're in power, you don't want it!') But none of us seriously believed that Liberals would soon have the opportunity to develop their policies in the form required by a government in power.

However, it can be claimed that the Committee had explored the dimensions of an idea for reform in tax and distribution policy in advance of its time. I did what I could in later publications to keep the idea alive and now and again it has been taken out and dusted down and modifications suggested, the latest being the introduction by the Chancellor of the Exchequer, then a certain Gordon Brown, of part of the scheme through the making of positive payments to wage earners whose incomes are accounted for through the PAYE income tax system and are below the tax exemption limit — over half a century later! (The National Insurance system, however, has remained virtually untouched.)

Between then and now, a tax reform was investigated at the request of the Tory Government of the early 1970s, though their fall in 1974 put paid to any further consideration of it. Interestingly enough, it had quite a wide remit covering the amalgamation of a number of social security benefits, including those provided through the National Insurance scheme with proposals to reform the exemptions allowed under the income tax system. A Green Paper (Cmnd Paper No 5142, 1973) outlining the reform scheme was published. In March 1973, the newly-formed Institute of Fiscal Studies ran a conference on the proposals and I was asked to contribute, along with several academics—Tony Atkinson, Brian Abel-Smith, Alan Prest, Alan Maynard (my co-author) and David Piachaud. On this occasion, the Inland Revenue sent a Study Group to explain the administrative changes that would be required, and their paper may fairly be described as much more positive than that which confronted us in 1951.[1]

I was pleased that it was now possible to bring further to light the importance of looking at badly-needed reforms in the welfare state, from a liberal point of view, and shall say much more about this general issue at a later stage. There was a particular point about drawing attention to this episode in the history of the development of economic thought on social policies, now a subject, not so in my early professional career, much in vogue with social scientists. The designer of the Green Paper was none other than FA (by this time Sir Arthur) Cockfield who, in a previous career as a public official, had done so much to sink our earlier Liberal attempts to promote the same kind of scheme—a paradox indeed! Some readers will recognise him as (later) Lord Cockfield, who became Vice President of the European Community, reaching the pinnacle of a second career as *un homme d'affaires*.

There is one personal matter left hanging in the air during the giving of our oral evidence. Sir Arthur had asked the Commission to excuse me if I had to slope off in the middle of it. As I have explained, the long drawn-out questioning left no time for me to aid our delegation in the wider discussion of our support for the abolition of the existing system of National Insurance. I already had another set of inquisitors to face the same day, being called for a competitive interview for the vacant post of Reader in Public Finance at the

[1]   The papers were published as Publication No 5 of the Institute of Fiscal Studies, 1973, entitled *Conference on Proposals for a Tax-Credit System*.

London School of Economics. The interviewing board consisted of my senior professorial colleagues and, as the post
was a university appointment, it was chaired by the then
Vice Chancellor, the formidable Dame Lilian Penson (rather
irreverently known as Cocktail Lil). Initially, I was much
more nervous facing this second group, but Dame Lilian
began by remarking on the fact that she gathered that I had
just been giving evidence to RCTPI, and asked me how I had
fared. If designed to put me at my ease, she was successful
indeed, and I gave a somewhat racy account of what had
happened. My colleagues, who included James Meade, one
of the pioneers in the whole field upon which our suggested
reforms were based, seemed less formidable than they had
appeared to be when, in 1948, they had interviewed me for a
Lectureship, but their questions were still as pointed.

An exhausting day ended with the welcome news (to me)
that I was to be offered the appointment.

Chapter 7

# *The Unservile State*

### I: Early Attempts at Advice-Giving

As explained in Chapter 2, the world of economic advice-giving has changed, and describing that change can reveal much about the conduct of political business. Today, the offering of such advice is 'institutionalised'. Whether one operates as an independent adviser or as a member of some advice-giving body such as a think tank or a Government committee, there is a distinct element of formality in the proceedings. The adviser presents a paper, circulated in advance. It is presented at a meeting with some person of authority in the Chair. Those who will process such advice sit round a table, their function being to raise questions. Depending on the status of the adviser, he or she may be listened to respectfully and on-the-spot criticisms are muted and tactful or, at the other extreme, the paper may be prepared by someone down the line who may have to suffer the criticism of their superiors, who expect the author to take it on the chin. The introduction of the paper into the production process of advice-giving depends on whether the author will be asked for revisions. Whether or not the paper will be published, and in a form of which the author approves, is a matter of his/her contract with those who take the final decision on its fate. Minutes of meetings will be recorded, circulated, revised and filed. The adviser, having fulfilled the contract, will then be paid, or retained as an employee. Of course, there are many variants of the advice-giving process, but the general idea is clear enough.

Going back to the early 1950s with this description of one's current experience seems like a journey back into the world of primitive man. The demand for economic advice provided by economists could be a fairly modest amount of the input appearing in the briefing of a politician or, indeed, a senior civil servant; and the appointment of professional consultants, either on contract or as employees, was unusual. Of course, things had moved somewhat faster in the degree of appreciation of economists' skills, largely as a result of their contribution to the conduct of the war economy. If we go back a few years before then, we can recall the amusing account given by Winston Churchill, when Chancellor of the Exchequer, of his summoning the economist RG Hawtrey to his presence:

> the man should be released from the dungeon in which we were said to have immured him, have his chains struck off and the straw brushed from his hair and clothes to be admitted to the light and warmth of argument in the Treasury Boardroom.[1]

My colleagues, notably Lionel Robbins, James Meade and Richard Sayers—all previously deeply involved in the prosecution of the war economy—were frequently consulted by influential politicians, high-ups in finance and senior civil servants. I had become the lineal successor of Hugh Dalton, who was one of Churchill's cabinet during WW2 and the Labour Chancellor of the Exchequer after it. Reader in Public Finance at LSE in the 1920s and 1930s, he had taught Lionel and could claim to have been largely responsible for Lionel's appointment as Professor. As well as being an influential Labour activist in that period, he had an enviable academic reputation at home and abroad for his publications on fiscal questions. If the propinquity of LSE to the seat of government encouraged such informal contacts, they were closely rivalled by Oxford, where a much more deliberate attempt was made to influence policy, as with the establishment of Nuffield College. I am told that

[1]    See Henry Roseveare, *The Treasury*, Allen Lane, Penguin Press, 1969, p. 27. Hawtrey wrote some widely respected books on monetary theory and policy.

DN Chester,[2] Warden of Nuffield, was so taken with the mission of influencing government that when he visited London, he dressed as a senior civil servant, down to the wearing of a bowler hat and carrying a rolled umbrella! The examples display an aspect of the interchange of political ideas, not obviously confined to this country, by which policy is formed out of private whispered conversations, which may be as influential as careful consideration, by politicians and civil servants, of the conclusions found in publicly available reports by Royal Commissions and their modern equivalents.

My introduction to Liberal politics through the Report on Income Tax and Social Security was the beginning of a passage from being a number-cruncher with a few ideas to that of a minor 'guru', brought out occasionally to help Liberal MPs and members of the House of Lords with puzzling out such matters as the meaning and significance of the annual budgets. The Report may have been an introduction to the dilemmas of relating economic analysis to acceptable policies, but not to the peregrinations one was called upon to make in becoming more directly involved with policy formation and presentation.

As already pointed out, 50 years ago being an MP had the appearance of being a part-time occupation and that was, in important aspects, a reality. This was immediately obvious to me because the several meetings I attended with MPs were not held in some office of theirs in the House of Commons. Richard Wainwright, whom I got to know very well

---

[2]   I must admit to being in debt to Chester for his help with contacts on national insurance matters when preparing my first book which grew out of my 1949 article. He had been Secretary for the famous Beveridge Report. He wrote a thousand word review of that book in Public Administration, of which he was Editor, damning it without a touch of faint praise. I was so concerned about the consequences of this that I apologised to my publisher. I learnt two things from this experience. The first was that damnation in one academic quarter might be a recommendation in another. The second was that publishers are less likely to care what is said about a book than be impressed by the eminence of the reviewer and the length of the review. Far from being upset, Mr Michael of Wm Hodge and Co was delighted!

before he became an MP, used to explain his position as rather like that of being a new schoolboy when he was first elected to the House. He barely had room to hang up his coat, but he did manage to find a locker into which he could stuff his papers; and that was some years after the early 1950s. Whatever the case for preventing our political system from being regarded as a long-term and sole career, encouraging a strategy of trying to maximise the length of one's life in office with the prospect of some prestigious sinecure on retirement, the provision of an office for our legislators does not now seem an extravagance.

My peregrinations were a consequence of this paucity of facilities, together with the very limited resources that the Liberal Party could now provide for the use of its own administration. In the course of the next five years, before I moved from London in 1956,[3] I was asked to meet the few remaining Liberal MPs, typically on an individual basis. It usually involved asking me questions about something I may have written for the *Manchester Guardian*, still then sympathetic to the Liberal cause, and the *Banker*, where its Editor, Wilfrid King, kept the tradition alive that economics should penetrate the skulls of ignorant and arrogant holders of high office. Meetings of this sort were held in the most unusual places, increasing my knowledge of the geography of the side alleyways of central London. The *Manchester Guardian* office, itself not far from LSE, was tucked away somewhere off Fleet Street, where Richard Fry, its City Editor, and his then Assistant Bill Clarke would always have time for a chat when one might be delivering the occasional copy or idea for an article. Pubs were a common venue, notably St Stephen's Tavern, then a favourite watering hole within the sound of the Division Bell in the House of Commons. Sometimes one might be able to return their hospitality by a cup of coffee at LSE, balanced on their knees in the cramped space of my little office. A step-up would be

---

[3] I was offered the Chair of Economic Science at the University of Edinburgh, an opportunity hardly to be missed with Chairs in those days scarce indeed. I accepted and returned to Scotland. Its consequences are considered in the next chapter.

the National Liberal Club, which I was later to join, with meetings taking place in some odd corner of the Smoking Room where the dingy wallpaper was coming away from the plastering, in contrast to its beautiful curved staircase, restored with the proceeds of War Damage Compensation. The high point of these conspiratorial gatherings was to be invited to lunch by the colourful and engaging Liberal leader, Philip Fothergill, and to his favourite restaurant, The Ivy, a rare occasion indeed even during my long lifetime.[4]

Most of these encounters in strange locations were increasingly with Jo Grimond, which requires me to take a step backwards in time to explain our connection. I have no record of any of these occasions, but they all point towards the extension of my thinking about liberal matters in my 'popular' writing, and particularly as a member of the Unservile State Group (USG). The Group grew out of an amalgam of committed Liberals and independent liberals, primarily but not exclusively academics (mainly from Oxford), with Elliot Dodds, Editor of the *Huddersfield Examiner*, its founder, then Vice-Chairman and later Chairman of the Liberal Party. It began meeting in 1953 in Oxford and then in London.

A crucial factor in its foundation was an informal get-together of Liberal MPs and candidates together with a small group of academics. I cannot recall the exact time and place of this affair but it must have been over a weekend in the Parliamentary summer recess in 1950 and, unsurprisingly, took place in a down-at-heel Bayswater hotel.

It was not an unmitigated success. The academic line-up included George Allen (Oxford Agricultural Economics,

---

[4]   When I became Reader in Public Finance, on two occasions I invited Hugh Dalton, my predecessor in the post, to talk to graduate students. Taking him afterwards to lunch at the National Liberal Club involved walking up the wonderful new staircase. He looked wistfully around him as we proceeded past several members who were amazed and possibly disturbed by his presence amongst them. He smiled and, in his well-known booming voice observed: 'I was once a member of this Club. I recollect that in those days it was called the Club where English is occasionally spoken and the nailbrushes in the toilets have to be chained to the wall'!

Fellow of St Edmund Hall, Oxford), Graeme Dorrance
(Canadian economist, Lecturer in International Economics
at LSE), Neville Ward-Perkins (Economist, Fellow of
Pembroke College, Oxford), Peter Wiles (Economist, Fellow
of New College, Oxford) and myself. The reception that we
received from the hardened politicians, notably Lady Violet
Bonham Carter, Clement Davies, Tony Stodart, and Lady
Megan Lloyd George was one of weary scepticism. We were
all in a vulnerable position, not realising that we were providing the main contributions. There is nothing more open
to attack by experienced politicians (especially the lawyers
amongst them) than the written word of others, particularly
concerning economic policy. We had all made a deliberate
attempt to link academic thinking on liberalism to the practical issues of the moment, but by the end of the meetings
one had the impression that we had failed to establish that
link and even that we were somehow not entitled to try.

My own contribution, built on the experience of having
taken part in the social security reform proposals, is already
explained in detail. The general reaction to it offered the
clear impression that there were good practical reasons for
avoiding its discussion. However, well received as the
RITSS had been, the small group of Liberal MPs and their
supporters in the House of Lords were more intent on capi-
talising on the high public reputation of William Beveridge
and his Report, and particularly as he had chosen to sit in
the upper house as a *Liberal* peer. They could hardly accept a
Report which questioned the whole basis of the national
insurance system, as, indeed, had my longer version which
was to be published in 1952.[5] A more specific but rather
mysterious criticism was advanced by no less a figure than
Lady Vi herself. She was surprised that I had not considered
the importance of proportional representation as the key-
stone of the method for electing our MPs. I replied that my
paper hardly required me to do so, whatever my own personal views on the matter were, not being an expert on the
appraisal of voting systems. I had incautiously added that

[5]   See *Economics of National Insurance,* Wm. Hodge, 1952, and the
      reference to the review by Chester mentioned above.

my paper 'was not intended to be comprehensive in content'. She whipped back a reproof which it would be difficult for anyone to forget: 'A contribution to our policies that does not *comprehend* proportional representation is of little use to me.'

While accepting the logic of rejection of social security reform, and the 'time is not yet ripe' argument applied to complementary reforms suggested by other speakers, we were united, I seem to remember, in our opposition to the continuance of Liberal support for the protection of agriculture, at least in the form of discrimination against foreign imports. Mr Stodart, Liberal candidate for the rich pastures and uplands of East Lothian, was scathing about Free Trade. (I preferred the honest sound of vested interests revealed by Mr Jones, a Liberal candidate in High Barnet in his advertisement in our local weekly newspaper: 'What this country needs is Free Trade and Sound Money', below which was written: 'Order only through your UK agent: Buy British.' Mr Jones as an importer was clearly in favour of Imperial Preferences.) Mr Stodart left the Liberal Party shortly afterwards, joined the Tories and became a Conservative MP. As is well known, Lady Megan, together with Dingle Foot, former Liberal MP for Dundee, joined the Labour Party.

This sort of uncomfortable episode in one's career has to be put down to experience. It was not entirely a negative one. Lady Vi's son-in-law was present and took a definite interest in what was discussed. He was to form a long association with our group, when it had licked its wounds and became reconstituted under the leadership of Elliot Dodds ... but that is another story. His name, by the way, was Jo Grimond.

## II: Rounding up the Academics

Elliot Dodds clearly believed that, whatever the short-term political situation might be, some clearer statement of Liberal policies based on liberal principles needed to be prepared. A beginning had been achieved with the RITSS but it only covered the economics of social policy and only some aspects of that. However, it had set a good precedent as to how principles and policies could be matched and, thanks to Guy Naylor, avoided the growing tendency to wrap up political economy in technical jargon, impenetrable to a wide public. Elliot set up the Unservile State Group[6] (USG) in 1953 based in Oxford (where most of the chosen members resided) with 'outliers' in London. From its inception, it included, as with RITSS, a strong connection with the Liberal Party, but unlike RITSS, included a Liberal MP, no less a figure than Jo Grimond, shortly afterwards to become Leader in the Liberals in the House of Commons. However, it was always clear that the Group had no formal connection with the Party. This became an important rider for it enabled the Group to invite independent, liberally-minded thinkers to join its ranks and later in its history these included Sam Brittan and Jack Wiseman.

Adam Smith voiced his suspicions of those who formed cosy little groups for, in the case of business people, 'diversion and merriment' could end up with 'a conspiracy against the public'. Gatherings of academics are not generally successful in affecting the welfare of their fellowmen and may even pride themselves for holding discussions specifically designed to be of no practical use whatsoever. Agreement at the end of such gatherings is more likely to be a confession of failure and success guaranteed only by reaching a crescendo at their conclusion leading to 'a tumult of voices'.

Elliot Dodds therefore had a job on his hands, if he was to get such a Group to produce a range of policies to fill his ambition of being the first full scale study of British Liberal thinking since the Yellow Book of 1928, particularly associated with Keynes and Lloyd George. He did not have to worry about the demand for such a study, for there was

[6]   Elliot traced the origin of this title to the labelling of the upstart radicals in the Spanish Cortes of 1810 as 'Liberals', that is as insubordinate and 'unservile' (see *The Unservile State; Essays in Liberty and Welfare*, Allen and Unwin, 1957, p. 13). Actually, *The Servile State* is the title of a once well-known attack on state interference published by Hilaire Belloc in 1912.

already intense debate in progress on the impact of Labour's nationalisation programmes and systems of physical controls. Engendering supply was a different matter. There was a wide field to cover. Potential writers, notably younger academics, had only recently embarked on their careers, already interrupted by WW2, and had academic and research obligations, not to speak of young families, which competed for their time. Graham Hutton, a famed freelance economist, had the advantage of experience and, despite a busy career as an independent journalist and consultant, wielded a fluent pen for the Liberal cause. Elliot faced the strain of having to move about between London, Huddersfield and Oxford and his being Vice President of the Liberal Party was no sinecure. Jo Grimond, only a few years launched into his remarkable political career, had even more logistic problems as the recently elected MP for Orkney and Shetland. So if the Group were to produce anything worth competing with, say, Tony Crosland's pathbreaking *Economics of Socialism* (Cape, 1956), which was nearing completion, someone was needed to ensure that the result combined the virtues of clarity, depth and originality as well as a sufficient joint commitment to an agreed definition of Liberalism. That 'someone' would have to possess the intellectual authority and personality to be able to get authors to review their own work crucially as well as the proverbial patience of a saint. Who was it to be?

Before answering that question, mention must be made of a mystery attaching to the membership of the USG. One of the close associates of Elliot Dodds had been Arthur Seldon, later to become very well known as one of the founders of the Institute of Economic Affairs (IEA) in 1955. About the time of the outbreak of WW2, Seldon was recruited to help with the research and drafting which led to the publication of *Ownership for All*, a report prepared by a committee which Elliot chaired. The report was a truly radical document which described the distribution of property in the UK as so unequal as to be 'gross and shocking'. For me, the most interesting feature of this document is its attempt to provide a market solution to the problem and to utterly

reject public ownership of property. Policy should have as
its main objects

> to create the legal structure in which a free economy can
> function; to see that the market is efficient and honest; to
> outlaw restraint of trade; to break down unjust and artifi-
> cial privileges; to preserve the national resources ... to
> maintain and expand the social services; and to place all the
> opportunities of a full life hitherto open only to the rich.

In a word, the Liberal view is that it is the function of the
State "to create the conditions of liberty".[7] Seldon retained
his connections with the Liberal Party until the 1950s. I
merely speculate on why he was not approached – he may
already have been too busy with the establishment of the
IEA, he may have been alienated – as I was later – by the
lack of response to his approach to policy, and he had certainly not changed his position from that of the early 1940s
before he became a war-time soldier. He could well have
written on the economics of the welfare and state with his
practised pen, his gift for exposition and his commitment – and performing better than I was able to with my
limited experience. I can only claim that my 'anxiety to do
good' was nurtured without knowing until very recently
how far Arthur's commitment went back in time. Unfortunately, I cannot ask either Elliot or Arthur for Elliot died in
the 1970s and Arthur quite recently.

The Group first met in 1953 but *The Unservile State : Essays
in Liberty and Welfare* (Allen and Unwin) did not appear
until 1957. That it appeared at all, and produced as a cooper-
ative effort, is primarily due to George Watson, its Editor.
George was a research fellow in English Literature at
Oxford and already a committed and active Liberal. Given
that the Group were to produce an agreed Report, he had
first of all to contend with the individualism of the academics who sought some form of personal recognition for con-

---

[7]    Quoted from 'Liberals and the New Right' by John Meadowcroft and
       Jaime Reynolds, *Journal of Liberal History*, Summer 2005, pp. 48–49. I
       am glad to acknowledge the debt I owe to these authors and also to
       conversations with John Meadowcroft, now Editor of the IEA's
       *Journal of Economic Affairs* and Lecturer in Public Policy at King's
       College, London.

tributions that were expected to advance Liberal thought. His second problem was to see that all the writers avoided jargon and wrote in plain English, often about complicated issues. He solved the first problem, which was agreed by all of us as an acceptable compromise, that we could append our initials to those contributions for which we were mainly responsible. The second entailed a combination of tact, persuasion and genial brutality of editing with no quarter given. It all took time, but I believe that the effort was worth it. Typically, none of the contributions has his initials at the end of it, but any fluency in writing and consistency of argument, both within individual contributions and as a collective effort is largely due to him.

My own contribution is an extension of the idea that the dilemma of a clash between liberty and equality may be resolved, if never completely, by following the method of the Classical economists in viewing the market and the state as alternative methods of allocating resources.

However, in response to the need to produce policy proposals that were directly related to social policies already put in place by the Labour Government, I geared my contribution to this requirement; and this produced a fortunate complementarity between my current policy research already offered to the academic marketplace. In this respect, I gladly threw my lot in again with Frank Paish and we wrote a series of joint articles, a substantial one in the LSE 'house' journal in Economics — *Economica* — on what we called 'The Economics of Dependence, 1952–82' (*Economica*, Vol 21(4) 1954), in *Lloyds Bank Review* (October 1954) and in the *Manchester Guardian* (February 7 and 8, 1955) on the cost of pensions, and which drew attention to the economic consequences of the growth of industrial pensions. I wrote separately an article strongly criticising the Earnings Rule, which only allowed pensioners to earn £2 a week, anything above that amount being liable to tax, at the margin, at 100%! (see *Manchester Guardian*, May 1956).

Alongside this flurry of activity, I had already acquired a separate modest reputation as a specialist on the economics of social policy, my 'political' interests not being regarded by colleagues as a barrier between me and the truth, but regarded by them with amused tolerance. One result which is perhaps of interest was to be selected by the Royal Economic Society (RES) to give a paper on the problems of the social services, at a discussion headed by Lord Beveridge himself, to whom were added the 'heavyweights' SP Chambers (see Chapter V) and Colin Clark, with yours truly taking up the rear to speculate on the future as displayed in my number-crunching exercises. The official RES Minute of that meeting held at the conclusion of its 1954 AGM is reproduced as Annex 7.1, together with my paper which has remained unpublished until now. Perhaps it gives something of the flavour of how the social services began to become more important in the economists' agenda compared with the days when I first started to study them. The last sentence of the summary of my contribution is revealing — my recognition of the importance of the interdependence between changes in the standard of living and changing perceptions of the standards required in social services provision.

### III: Had the Unservile State any Influence?

Influence of the ideas and arguments in contributions such as those in *The Unservile State* are difficult to detect, far less to measure. I have known think tanks, and individual pundits, claim that their 'clothes have been stolen' by other organisations. A simple technique is to list a series of one's 'original' proposals alongside those that have actually become common currency in the understanding and influence of public figures and, better still, are sanctified in their adoption as the law of the land. But, as we warn our students, correlation must not be confused with causation. It is virtually impossible to establish a copyright in economic ideas and policies, that being one reason why, if an idea becomes accepted but proves to be wrong, with some result which affects the material fortunes of those that accept it, it is probably impossible to sue the progenitor. While this may let the economist off the hook, it removes a barrier to entry into the market of ideas which encourage those with no training in economics thinking to enter the market, usually for the purpose of attracting attention to dramatic statements about the economic future. Natural scientists, even of great distinction in their own field of enquiry, are prone to fall into the temptation of doing so, as some of their recent apocalyptic statements about global warming offer striking evidence. As a liberal, I have to accept this situation 'with a patient shrug', for I would oppose the acceptance by the State of a petition which, if successful, would allow economists to decide who in law was to be able to practise their trade.

Despite these misgivings about the promulgation of economic ideas, listed below are the main conclusions of my own contribution which took the form of suggestions for inclusion in any Liberal programme of reform:

a.   A full scale investigation of the present and future economic condition of the aged with a view to reforming the existing structure of pensions.

   (Comment: Today this looks like a statement of the obvious, but it was not so in the 1950s when, with hardly any time for the Labour Government to get something like the Beveridgean system in place, radical reform would not be in prospect. Since then, less than a decade has gone by without investigation of changes in the system, usually accompanied by economic and social studies which have kept many a university Department of Economics and of Social Policy busy on research, much of it supported by the various Rowntree Trusts. They have been very much to the fore during the entire half-century since the USG was set up. Much later I was to be closely involved in the design of reform of pensions as a member of the Fowler Committee (see c. below). The culmination of this concern over the magnitude of the problem of the aged is instanced in the establishment of the Pensions Policy Institute in the late 1990s, which, in order to keep a watchful eye on policy changes, has to maintain an almost weekly running commentary on what these would entail.)

b.  Notwithstanding a., the immediate abolition of the earnings limit for retirement pensions and widows' benefits.

(Comment: I have reprinted my article in the *Manchester Guardian* written prior to the appearance of the *Welfare Society* (see Annex 7.3). It sets out in detail my objections to this relic from depression economic thinking that influenced Beveridge, although he was not disposed to defend the limit, as my article indicates. I offer only the observation that after years of campaigning, the limit was finally abolished over 40 years later!)

c.  Measures to increase the transferability of pension rights. One method would be to remove the tax privileges afforded to these schemes from those which are financed solely by an employer's contribution.

(Comment: The question of the limits imposed on transferability of pension rights by both the attempt of major industrial interests to raise the cost to employees wishing to work elsewhere than in their present employment and by the tax treatment of pension rights was to become a major issue in pensions policy. It arose particularly when, in the 1950s, the Labour Government seriously proposed the extension of national insurance pensions to create a 'dynamic' state pensions system. This would require the introduction of compulsory contributions related to income level designed to finance state pensions related to final salary. However, such a scheme would involve a radical extension of the power of government with existing and potential occupational pensions contracts between employers and the employed. I was originally alerted to the difficulties that would arise by Frank Paish and during our collaboration in the articles mentioned above (p. 93) My experience in helping to devise a personal pensions scheme as put forward by the Fowler Committee in the mid 1980s is laid out in my article in the *Economic Journal*, No 3, 1992. This article offers pensions policy as an example of the practical difficulties in devising consistent economic policies as discussed earlier in Chapter 2. I believe that it remains true to liberal principles!)

d.  The abolition of all food and housing subsidies.

(Comment: This proposal clearly indicates the expansion of my interests to consider distributional issues in a much wider context than pensions. The differences between liberals and democratic socialists over distribution lay less in the matter of the degree of redistribution required as a result of continuing inequality of incomes and of wealth and more in the form such measures should take. Liberalism requires that more equality must not be bought at the cost of a reduction in personal liberty. Therefore, if poverty is a barrier to the purchase of goods perceived as necessary for decent living and enjoyment, then income support must be the answer and not price support of particular goods and services. Moreover, the regulation and provision of price subsidies place much more power in the hands of government departments and agencies than in the case of generalised income support, which can conflict with personal liberty. Of course, this argument needs to be much more fully developed and illustrated by actual experience, and this is attempted later. The case of education and equality merits separate treatment and plays a much more direct part in my ultimate failure to 'do good' — see e. below, and Chapter 8.)

e.  The introduction of some form of tax relief to those who choose to educate their children privately, related perhaps to the direct cost per child educated in state institutions.

(Comment: This proposal — and its development into a more radical voucher system to finance all school education, whether publicly or privately provided — was a real test of the willingness of politicians to face up to the problem of reconciling liberty and equality. It brought me to the fore of policy discussion at the party level, and ultimately resulted in my 'downfall' and withdrawal from both active politics and the Liberal Party itself. Whether the story is worth the telling is for the reader to judge, and the following chapters provide the material for doing so.)

Before endeavouring to deal with the question at the head of this section, an obvious pointer towards an answer is to examine the reaction of reviewers of the volume. There was a disappointingly mild reaction from the quality press, apart from the friendly *Manchester Guardian*, probably because our attempt to link our contribution to the Yellow Book of the 1930s was hindered by the lack of contemporary understanding as to what the Yellow Book had stood for. We would be bound to take particularly seriously the views in professional publications including *The Economist*. I offer three examples of professional reactions.

The first is a review by Arthur Shenfield, then becoming a prominent 'free market' economist of a kind more familiar in the United States. In *Economica* (August 1958, pp. 266–77) — of which I had been Assistant Editor (see Chapter 3) — he displayed his considerable skill as a Hayekian disciple, and subjected our work to a brief rigorous analysis. He was severely critical of the analysis in Elliot Dodds', Wiles' and Peacock's essays trying to reconcile liberty and equality through reform of the welfare state. (He differentiated between the 'originality' of Wiles and the 'skill' of Peacock!) He stuck rigidly to the view that any form of redistribution of income — a necessary consequence of the development of the welfare state — was an attack on liberty. I found this to be highly questionable. In the first place, as I was increasingly pointing out, an attack on individual decision making as a consequence of state provision could be avoided insofar as state outlays to support individuals were given in the form of cash. In the second place, Shenfield must have been assuming that the personal distribution of income and capital would be optimal *sans* welfare state provision, which was necessarily a value judgement not possible to derive from economic analysis. However, one must be thankful that, in the last analysis and taking account of his mild approval of the other contributions on politics, industrial policy, colonial affairs, education and land reform, he was to conclude that: 'The result is a symposium on the problems of our time which, despite defects, which are not negligible, is marked by a perceptiveness high above the normal level of political party publications.' Used to savage reviews in academic journals, Shenfield seems mild in comparison.

Earlier, the proposition was announced that the more prestigious a journal regarded itself, the less likely that the reviewer's name would be revealed. There is this only one occasion when I felt that *The Economist*, which used this practice, has reviewed anything of mine unfairly. In fact, that of my first book (see p. 64 above) was positively laudatory! However, the reviewer on the occasion of the appearance of our volume seemed to regard us as writing a requiem for the Liberal Party. He passed the magisterial judgement on our symposium that 'the creation of liberalism with its old party roots gone, (it) is precisely the disinterestedness that is its apparent virtue' (October 26 1957, p. 304). Wow! (No critical assessment was given of any individual contribution.)

I found it more gratifying, and surprising, that our efforts were taken seriously by the now-famous Friedrich Hayek, who had left LSE suddenly in 1950 and was about to begin his long sojourn in the United States, where he wrote his famous series of highly influential works on the principles and practice of libertarianism. These works were a backcloth for a devastating critique of the claims of scientists to know the future and how the state could control it.

I happened to review the first of these works, *The Constitution of Liberty* (first published in England by Routledge and Kegan Paul, 1960), shortly after its appearance and came across two references to *The Unservile State*. The first, on p. 304, considers the claim by both Peter Wiles and Elliot Dodds that the welfare state was only a temporary phenomenon with the prospect that with the growth in wealth, it would become largely unnecessary. Hayek's reply was reminiscent of the pessimistic stance in his famous book, *The Road to Serfdom*, which appeared towards the end of WW2. He wrote: 'It must seem doubtful, however, whether there exists such a distinct phase of evolution in which the net effects of those monopolistic institutions are likely to be beneficial, and still more whether, once they have been created, it will ever be politically possible again to get rid of them.' One can concede to Hayek that there could be nothing automatic about a change in public attitudes to the welfare state which would render it unnecessary. This was one of the reasons why the criticised authors and myself had paid so much attention to the question as to what alternatives to government control over welfare could be made to appeal to the public and offer Liberal politicians a fresh approach to policy questions more in keeping with liberal principles. This debate about the possibilities of change still goes on, and how it developed since the late 1950s is a large part of what follows later in this work.

So far the 'Oxford Group', but the 'LSE Group' fared slightly better, although Nancy Seear's contribution on industrial relations was not considered by Hayek. It could fairly be claimed that the most appealing and persuasive contribution to *The Unservile State* was written by Graham Hutton, one-time lecturer at LSE, and well ahead of the youngsters with his vast experience as an industrial consultant, in the intellectual vigour and balance in his writing and in practical wisdom on economic policy. The appeal of his work to Hayek lay in Hutton's observation that high rates of progression in income tax brought in surprisingly little revenue from the rich. He could therefore agree with Hutton's conclusion that the solution to improving incentives to channel enterprise into better economic performance lay in the retention of income differentials and to transfer the fiscal burden, after ensuring greater efficiency in the operation of public sector services, to forms of taxation of inherited wealth.

I was more concerned with the illiberality of methods of income support which relied on direct subsidies on goods and services, that is to reducing their price (in some cases such as education) to zero. The preferred method for income redistribution, made necessary because the pre-tax distribution of income was considered 'unfair', was by some form of income transfers. Hayek noted that, along with Henry Simon, an eminent US fiscal theorist, I did not base this conclusion on the utilitarian belief that, as a matter of fact, an extra pound of income was 'more valuable' to the poor than to the rich. It rested on a positive dislike of income inequality (Hayek, *op. cit.* p. 518). He could accept it as an argument based on a value judgement, as I had done, though it is clear that Hayek did not agree with it. Unfortunately, no opportunity ever arose for me to discuss this point further with my former senior colleague.

One cannot assume that our conclusions led to the subsequent discussion during the rest of the 1900s, and in some cases actually adopted as government policy. Likewise, if one cannot assume that the balance of public reaction to our proposals, as instanced in reviews, was in our favour, what can be said in favour of them? If the external reaction was at least equivocal, there is clear evidence that the 'internal' reaction within the Liberal Party itself was positive; and that mattered quite a lot to most of the authors. The Parliamentary Party came to rely on the series of studies sponsored by the Group which could form the raw material of their own thoughts on how to relate academic thinking to their practical concerns. Moreover, it could stimulate politicians themselves to set this down in their own style and manner, a classic example being Jo Grimond's early attempt in *The Liberal Challenge* (Hollis and Carter, 1963). This book covers the whole spectrum of government policy and derives from his own perception of what the USG set out earlier, and provides a series of reforms ranging from fundamental changes in the structure of political decision making to its consequences for administrative reform. Jo was often criticised as being a little too relaxed, almost 'languid', in his approach to his task as Leader of the Party, as he was soon to become, but this certainly was not displayed in this exercise of his brainpower. Without his own efforts and example as thinker and writer, policy would have continued to lack both content and direction. Not surprisingly, his interest and enthusiasm for Elliot Dodds' invention and George Watson's steersmanship, was a major factor in attracting the attention of liberals outside the Party who could add lustre to the Group's later membership.

## Annex 7.1: Royal Economic Society 1954 AGM

*Current Topics*

The Annual Meeting of the Royal Economic Society was held at the London School of Economics on Thursday, June 24, 1954. Professor Lionel Robbins was elected to the office of President in succession to Lord Brand. Mr A.D. Marris was elected Treasurer in succession to Mr HC. Mynors, who had resigned the office on his appointment as Deputy-Governor of the Bank of England.

After the conclusion of the formal business there was a discussion of 'The Problems of the Social Services'. It was opened by Lord Beveridge, who had lately returned from the United States and emphasised the remarkable growth and widespread acceptance of social services of certain kinds in that country. He was glad that the British social services were being thoroughly investigated by the Guillebaud and Phillips Committees and by the Government Actuary. He was convinced that the right basis for them was insurance. He was concerned at the inadequacy of rates of benefit now provided and the increasing number of pensioners who had to have recourse to public assistance. But he was most anxious that the state services should be a minimum-subsistence basis, to which individuals would add by their own efforts.

Mr Colin Clark argued that expenditure on the social services was involving the nation both in much too high a level of taxation and in a centralisation of administration and a control of it by Parliament and the Civil Service which was in his view very undesirable. He was anxious to see a reversal of present trends and the administration of services wherever possible by nongovernmental bodies. He was pessimistic about the increase of national income, and feared that all the increase would be absorbed in raising services and none be available to reward extra effort.

Mr AT Peacock compared the national expenditure in some of the social fields with that before the war, and showed that the increase, though considerable, was not wholly disproportionate to the growth of national income.

He attempted a forecast of the level of expenditure at 1982. He predicted appreciable increase of expenditure on health, on the basis of present standards, but a very considerable increase on education and a decline of expenditure on housing after some ten years of further building at present rates. If national income continued to grow at 1½% per annum he did not think that the social services would confront us with grave problems. These would be the consequence, rather, of increases of standards above those now prevailing.

Mr SP Chambers disagreed with a suggestion of Mr Clark that the state could divest itself of responsibility for certain minimum standards. He argued that the state had long accepted this responsibility, and a democratic country could not go back on it. He suggested, however, that the finance of social services derived from compulsory contributions, which were in effect taxation, and that the ordinary criteria of equity required that the expenditure should be met from general taxation on a proportional or progressive basis rather than from a regressive tax.

In the subsequent discussion Professor Titmuss emphasised the immense importance both in the United States and in the United Kingdom of voluntary pension schemes, which were growing very fast, were now much more important than the state scheme and which disposed of very large investible funds.

## Annex 7.2: Paper delivered at AGM (previously unpublished), The Problem of the Social Services (III)

### I: Introduction

In preparing my part of the discussion, I have suffered the disadvantage of having to make some assumptions about the content of the contributions of the previous speakers. My main assumption was that they would spend most of their time talking about the political economy of social services rather than the economics. I find that my main assumption was right. I have no wish to query the propriety of discussing what ought to be done about our social policy, but I do think that at a meeting of the Royal Economic Society we should be prepared at some stage to substitute fairly rigorous economic analysis for highly vigorous political debate.

I propose, therefore, to take the social services as they are rather than as they ought to be, and to consider how far the objectives implied in their provision conform or conflict with what we loosely call our economic objectives. My talk falls naturally into two parts. The first considers the immediate past and the present position of the social services in our economy and their broad effects, and the second considers the probable consequences in the future of the continuance of the present standards of social service provision.

Before proceeding with any such analysis I must confess that there is a serious difficulty to be faced. We are becoming increasingly used to studies in applied economics of a dissective character in the field of industry, but for some reason the important industries of health and education have remained sadly neglected. Taking the articles in the *Economic Journal* alone, it is interesting to find that over the last 30 years out of over 1,000 articles and memoranda published, only ten have had any connection with the social services—that is, less than one per cent. Of these ten, only two have appeared since the war, when the debate has been at its height. This I am sure is not a reflection on editorial policy but on the interests of the contributors. Perhaps economists feel like the political economist in one of Peacock's novels, who met the educationist and remarked afterwards: 'His subject had no beginning, middle, nor end. It was education. Never was such a journey through the desert of the mind: the Great Sahara of intellect. The very recollection makes me thirsty'. Thus even in regard to the provision of relevant economic information it is difficult to provide more than tentative estimates.

## II: *The Present Position of the Social Services*

In the fiscal year 1953–54, the current expenditure on social services at all levels of government (excluding food subsidies) was 33% of total government expenditure as compared with 36% in 1937–38. However, between these two dates, government expenditure as a percentage of gross national product has risen, so that we find that the direct expenditure on goods and services (largely education and health) on social services has risen over the same period from 5% to 8% of the gross national product. If we consider social transfers (largely insurance and assistance payments), we find that they were 5% of total personal incomes before tax in 1937–38, 5.5% in 1950–51 and 6.5% in 1953–54. None of these indicators of growth in social services manifests very substantial changes. It is when we come to examine capital formation that we find a different picture. Capital expenditure on social services as a proportion of gross fixed capital formation rose from 10% in 1937–38 to 21% in 1953–54. Most of this expenditure was on housing.

I must add one paragraph more of statistics, for, in the end, it is the absorption of real resources by the social services, and the purchasing power of benefits which are economically significant. There are many technical difficulties in making any comparison with the situation before the war. Apart from the usual difficulties to be faced in constructing index numbers, such as the choice of weights and changes in quality, we do not have any precise information of the changes in the prices of goods and services absorbed by the social services. I have had to make a very rough guess at this, and I find that while the real national product per head has risen some 20% between 1938 and 1953, the increase in real expenditure on social services, by way of goods and services, seems to be somewhere about 30–35%. This calculation masks one very significant fact, and that is that between 1950 and 1953 it seems almost certain that the real expenditure per head on social services by way of goods and services has fallen. The same story holds for transfer payments. Apart from unemployment benefit, the purchasing power of social transfers rose, although not markedly, between 1938 and 1953, but if we take 1948 as a base year, the year of the introduction of the National Insurance system as we now know it, we find that the purchasing power of benefits has declined. I do not think that these figures are the ones which would seem to guide much popular discussion on social services provision.

What can we say about these developments? Is an increase in per capita expenditure of some 30–35% above the 1938 level in the provision of social services in the form of goods and services too much or too little? In the jargon of our subject, how do we determine the optimal level of expenditure on health and education? Economists are often expected to answer these questions, but I don't think that a few sentences in the *Economics of Welfare* elegantly embroidered in the *Economics of Control* are much to go on. I think we should give up the pretence of knowing what particular arrangements in society are better than others. Economics provides no answer to these questions so long as there is disagreement about the choice of objectives and their relative priority. Indeed, lack of recognition of this point has led to mistakes in economic analysis. You will often hear it argued that, given the objective of preventing inflation, social services are inflationary (and therefore they exceed the optimum level), and on the other hand, for instance by Professor Wootton, that the defence expenditure is the cause of inflation and not social services. Implicit in each of these positions is a judgement about policy. Obviously, given a situation of full employment of resources, then *any* additional government expenditure will be inflationary, other things being equal, but it is a matter of politics rather than economics whether you consider social services or defence expenditure as the marginal item.

But the same approach which I have criticised provides us with a useful framework of analysis when we take any given set of policy objectives. Thus with full employment of resources, the opportunity cost of social services can be measured in terms of the alternatives forgone, and one may very well be sceptical of government statements that we must re-equip our industries and release resources for export, then, at the same time, we increase the percentage of fixed capital formation on social services from (...) in a year of less-than-full employment, 1938, to over 20% in years of over-full employment. Moreover, the social services pro-vide other examples of the incompatibility of government objectives, when we turn from the allocation to the distribu-tion of current output. A policy of redistributing the claims on our national resources by providing public social ser-vices, largely at zero cost, to all, while at the same time pay-ing lip-service to an anti-inflationary policy, must mean that the whole weight of adjustment is thrown on the tax system. Whether or not one accepts Mr Clark's thesis that the crucial level of taxation is 25% of the national income, the fact remains that no one can seriously doubt the incom-patibility of heavy taxation with the demand for an expand-ing economy. I suppose that the obvious reply to this is that the social services are a form of investment in human capi-tal, an argument at least as old as Marshall, and one entitled to the utmost respect. However, we should need much more research to know how to translate either of these opposite effects into changes in the index of industrial pro-duction.

### III: *The Future of the Social Services*
When we look to the future, then the extent to which we can 'afford' social services involves assumptions about (a) the policy objectives of our economy and their translation into claims on our resources, and (b) the level of national pro-ductivity. Only an economist with the courage of a Colin

Clark would undertake a complete forecast. The most I shall attempt to do is to *project* present trends so that one assumes (a) the same policy objectives as at present, with the same priority of claims on the national resources, and (b) the same rate of increase in real national product as over, say, the period since the war.

We can now proceed on the basis of these assumptions to examine the impact of the social services on the economy of the future, given the *present standards of provision*. The method of procedure is to take some appropriate population projection, and relate our current standards of provision to the change in population structure. We know it to be roughly true, for instance, that the per capita expenditure on the health service is appreciably greater for those over 65 than those below. An ageing population, even given present standards of provision and with no change in the absolute total of population, would imply an increase in social services expenditure at current prices.

Here, then, are some very rough guesses based on these assumptions relating to the year 1982. Taking social transfers first, then, always given present rates of benefit, assuming little change in assistance payments, we could expect a rise of about 150% above the present level, largely because of the rise in pensions. There are all sorts of interesting facets to the pensions problem, but I cannot dwell on them here. All one can say is that some of the suggestions to reduce the pensions burden, such as raising the pensionable age for men and women on their own insurance would not be effective, because the bulk of the expenditure is for those over 70, and because a large part of total expenditure is for widows. Another interesting fact is that the change in costs is just as much due to changes in eligibility for benefit as to the age factor. Turning now to expenditure on goods and services, we should expect on our assumptions a considerable rise in expenditure on the health services, if we can judge from the present distribution of costs per age group for hospitals, and dental, pharmaceutical and ophthalmic services, although the published information here is very sketchy. I put this at about an extra 20%, although the population projection I have used puts the increase in total population at only **(?? )**. On the other hand, we should not expect education costs to rise, although some observers have been rather optimistic about the likelihood of a fall in expenditure on account of the slight fall in the school population. This does not take account of the expenditure per head in different age groups below 20. The other major item is housing. Here I think we can assume that it will be unnecessary to maintain the present rate of house-building beyond the present decade, even if we wish to raise standards to some extent. I think I have been generous in assuming capital expenditure at 1953 prices to be at about half the present rate. What this rough guess amounts to is an increase in social services expenditure at 1953 prices of about 12% to 15%, but this would largely be brought about by the increase in social transfers expenditure. The increase in expenditure on health services in the form of goods and services would be largely offset by the decrease in housing expenditure. A rise of 15% does not seem incompatible with even a modest rise in our national productivity over 30 years.

However, everything points to pressure for better standards of provision in all branches of the social services, and more immediately in the provision of higher pensions, as Lord Beveridge has pleaded. It might well be that our productivity will increase sufficiently to deal with this problem, which, as I have indicated, is largely a problem of supplying the needs of the aged. But as we persist in raising standards, however laudable this is, and insist on social services for all, then we may have to face a new form of class conflict—a conflict between the old and the young. This conflict will be made all the more acute by the fact that the rights of the old will be exercised to a large degree through the provision of state pensions, which implies, given pressure on resources, redistributory taxation. The payment of past contributions does not currently determine the ability to pay adequate pensions; it only provides the benefit in money terms as a right.

The interesting thing in all this for the economist is the extent to which the contemporary growth of state and industrial contributory pensions schemes may increase the net saving of the community, thus reducing the current claims on resources and so releasing resources for investment. The old of tomorrow would thus bring about the redistribution of resources necessary to provide themselves (or rather their widows) with sufficient to sustain them. There might thus be the case for an increase in the insurance contributions, particularly the employees' contribution, which, as poll-tax with only a very small tax relief for income tax, would increase saving. But this is only the Classical solution in a Keynesian disguise. In Keynesian terms, this would reduce the marginal propensity to consume, given the usual assumptions about the saving habits of different income groups; in Classical language it means increasing saving by increasing the inequality of income distribution. This is one approach, but it is not necessarily the most acceptable one.

**Annex 7.3:** *Manchester Guardian*, **4 May 1956**
**The Earnings Rule: Case for Abolition, by Alan Peacock**

There is a large body of official and unofficial opinion which accepts the Beveridge Report as holy writ. Quotation from this famous document is considered a substitute for reasoned argument. The report of the National Insurance Advisory Committee on the earnings limits for retirement pensions and widow's benefits, discussed in yesterday's *Manchester Guardian*, once again quotes reverently from the bible of the Welfare State, and represents a wasted opportunity for discussion of the whole rationale of the famous Beveridge 'retirement principle' which laid down retirement from work as a necessary condition in the granting of an adequate pension.

The committee itself cannot be blamed for the narrow terms of reference, for it was merely asked to consider what adjustment should be made in the present earnings limits. The possibility of querying the retirement principle and thus of considering the abolition of the limit was denied them. Perhaps the Minister of Pensions and National Insurance and his advisers forgot that Lord Beveridge himself was not disposed to defend the earnings limit when it was last considered officially by the Phillips Committee some eighteen months ago.

The details of the earnings limit are well known but the implications of it are not. From the point of view of equity there are serious anomalies which are difficult to rectify while economic considerations demand its immediate abolition. So far as equity is considered the fact that a retired person has his pension reduced by 1s for every 1s earned over £2 (£3 in the case of a widow) means that he or she is subjected to what is a marginal rate of tax of 100 per cent until the pension or benefit disappears. This tax is not an income tax; it is an earnings tax. Thus a retired person within the meaning of the National Insurance Acts who draws say £1 per week as the owner of rented property and a further £2 a week in gainful employment does not have his pension reduced but a person deriving the same income of

£3 from gainful employment alone will have his pension reduced by £1 a week.

## Anomalies

Again, no account is taken of fluctuations in earnings over the year: the limit is applied strictly on a weekly basis. A pensioner who takes a seasonal job and earns, say, £4 a week for three months will forfeit his pension for that period, but a man earning £2 a week for six months, the same aggregate sum, will lose nothing. In days when generous tax allowances are granted to industrial pension schemes and are promised to self-employed persons it seems anomalous to impose an earnings limit on a State retirement pension but not on industrial or Civil Service pensions — a point which Professor Titmuss and Miss Spelman stress in their brief note of dissent to the report.

The case in equity for the continuation of the earnings limit is not really discussed in the report, although some consideration is given to the question of averaging. As it is 'settled Government policy' (page 7) that pensions should be conditional on retirement, then the matter is decided for it. Given this criterion, then why raise the earnings limit at all? The truth of the matter is that Government policy is inconsistent. The earnings limit as envisaged in the Beveridge Report implied that pensions were adequate for subsistence. No supplementation would therefore be needed. If the Government refuses to raise pensions substantially (and there may be very good reason for this), then it cannot complain if there is pressure put upon it to remove disabilities to maintaining living standards by working.

The present policy may be one of the factors which encourage pensioners to increase their claims for national assistance. The usual reply to this argument is that under the present scheme the man of 65 who continues to work and pay contributions gets a higher pension as a result, while, if he reaches 70 and draws a pension, then no earnings limit is imposed. But if it is wrong in principle for a person both to draw a pension and remain in work then it is just as wrong at 70 as at 65, while it seems grossly inequitable to narrow the range of choice of the pensioner to one of either retiring altogether or of remaining in full-time employment.

In fact, the committee has accepted the trade union recommendation that the earnings limit should be raised a further 10s for pensioners to 50s. It is difficult to understand why the trade unions still insist on maintaining the earnings limit while they continue to demand the payment of retirement pensions as a right. This niggardly concession does not remove the curious illogicality of keeping the earnings limit 10s below that of widows under pensionable age, when wage rates for men are well above those for women, so that a higher limit for women enables a very considerable proportion of them to do a full week's work.

## Incentives

While the equity considerations weaken the case for a limit, economic considerations surely demand its abolition. With an ageing population our society faces the difficult problem of devising methods of encouraging older persons to continue at work which at the same time do not bar promotion to young persons by the refusal of the old to retire. A suitable compromise would produce systematic demotion of the old without a loss in status. More opportunities for part-time employment are what is required and a greater incentive to undertake work of this sort. As Professor Cairncross has argued in his reservation to the report of the Phillips Committee, 'It is desirable that men of 65–70 should be free to choose not whether to retire but how much to retire; far more desirable than that, every able-bodied man should postpone retirement until the last possible moment.' The abolition of the earnings rule would do something to achieve this objective.

There are two objections to this argument which have received a great deal of attention. There is our old friend, that abolition of the earnings limit will invite wage cutting by employers. It is hardly a respectable argument in days when trade union power and influence is widespread. It has no relevance to full employment conditions. The very strength of the trade unions in driving up wages may discourage rather than encourage employers to take on older persons. Indeed, there is a strong case for negotiating agreements in which employers, subject to safeguards, would be allowed to pay the standard rate of wages less the amount of the retirement pension to elderly persons and exempting employers from paying contributions in respect of those already drawing retirement pensions. This would encourage them to employ older persons who could not earn the standard wage.

The final argument is that the payment of an unconditional pension to all at 65 would be 'too expensive' to the National Insurance Fund even allowing for the fact that increased pensions to those who remained in full time employment would cease to be paid. The shadow of that mysterious computer the Government Actuary falls over the report, although its presence is only acknowledged in a footnote. We learn that the abolition of the retirement condition would cost the National Insurance Fund £76 millions a year immediately, although this figure would fall to £36 millions in 25 years' time. It is an interesting commentary on the power of the Actuary over the minds of successive committees that they take these figures as gospel.

Economists who endeavour to forecast our economic prospects have been dubbed astrologers by the Chancellor of the Exchequer, but if their assumptions seem extreme then the kind of assumption required by the Actuary to forecast retirement trends is entitled to be called necromancy. But even if the Actuary's figures were not called in question there need not be cause for alarm. The capacity of the nation to pay retirement pensions and widows' benefits does not depend on some narrow view of the finance of the National Insurance scheme based on a false analogy with private insurance. It depends on our national productivity. Although the abolition of the earnings limit might not have an appreciable effect on production immediately it will certainly do much in the long run as our population ages.

Moreover, the Treasury would recoup some revenue from the increased expenditure of pensioners.

The extraordinary thing about the discussion of the present and future pensions problem is that it is being conducted without any supporting inquiry into the economic resources of the aged. Sensible policies will not be formulated unless we have much mare information about the present and likely future economic conditions of the old. Mr Macmillan made specific reference in his Budget speech to the need for better economic information. Here is a ready-made and important problem which justifies full-scale investigation.

In short, the nature of the problems of the social services in the future will depend on whether or not we anticipate marked increases in the standard of service, for, given modest increases and present productivity trends, there seems to be little to fear.

# Chapter 8

# *Illusions of Influence*

## I: Moving away from the Political Coalface

The Unservile State Group was formed in 1955, *The Welfare Society* was published in 1957, Hayek's comment in his *Constitution of Liberty* three years later, and my review of it in 1961. By the following year, 1962, I had already been Professor of Economic Science in the University of Edinburgh for nearly six years, but was about to leave that ancient foundation for the then youngest university in the UK, York, where I became the foundation Professor of Economics. Much had happened during this period which requires a re-tracing of steps before explaining how, increasingly, involvement in Liberal economic and social policy led to my self-inflicted exile from having anything directly to do with the Liberal party's future.

From the LSE promotion in October 1951 to departure to occupy the Edinburgh Chair in December 1956 saw a vast change in the magnitude and direction of intellectual effort. It became no longer necessary to identify paths to follow in seeking to become a 'practitioner', and requests for what services I could offer came thick and fast. Only 29 at the beginning of this period and 34 when I went to Edinburgh, in retrospect succumbing to the temptation of believing one was fully trained and properly experienced was a mistake. While I was replete with ideas, my judgement on which were worth pursuing had not properly matured, and my technical skills did not measure up to a subject in which analytical progress was undergoing rapid change. It was like being the founder and Managing Director of a small firm which had managed to get a toehold in an ideas market and suddenly found itself drowning in orders.

The reconciliation of a claimed commitment to trying to do good had to take place between the requirement of subjecting research to the judgement of peers and yet at the same time working in a research area which had spin-offs for the improvement in welfare from a liberal standpoint. This turned out to be less of a problem than I had expected.

First of all, I decided that my foot soldiering days were over and I would now no longer take a direct part in local and national elections, except for occasionally speaking for a candidate. I had taken part in forays in the front line of politics, and came to admire the skill and dedication of local organisers of all parties. I spoke several times in Hornchurch for Nancy Seear before she was adopted as a candidate for Truro, and for Gershon Ellenbogen. But the distance from North Finchley to Hornchurch was quite forbidding, especially on foggy winter nights, and cost me time which would have been better spent with a young and growing family. The organisation of the heckling of candidates — remember the importance of public meetings before radio and television became methods for the transmission of political propaganda — was a practised art amongst organisers for all parties, although egregious unknown persons might spring up in an audience sometimes, causing trouble. I once accompanied the Hornchurch Liberal organiser to a meeting of the Tory Parliamentary candidate, a Mr Wentworth Day, who had a particular obsession about the importance of replacing the products of modern chemistry in improving crop yields with natural manure. One could guarantee that at the hustings a planted question would be put to him, which enabled him to offer a somewhat lengthy exposition on his pet theme. On one such occasion, our agent suddenly sprang up and shouted, 'Vote for Day and more dung!' His loyalists were furious, more so because it brought out a flood of laughter. Bouncers descended on us, and we fled before our exit could be hastened by strong arm tactics.

Occasional platform speaking was less of a strain, and invitations were probably extended because I had by then become a professor, once regarded as representing some kind of public as well as academic distinction. Whilst in Edinburgh, I spoke twice for William Douglas Home, then a very popular playwright with, quoting Noel Coward, "a talent to amuse". The second occasion was the 1962 election, when he hoped to move from being runner-up, as in the previous election, to being an MP. I cannot think that he was his own best friend, and two events served to mar his chances.

On the first, he persuaded Compton Mackenzie (Monty), who for some reason had quarrelled with the Scottish Nationalists, as a bosom friend to speak for him. For some reason he believed that I would be a crowd puller in South Edinburgh, and I was likewise seduced into supporting him. We mounted a teacher's dais in East Preston Street Primary School, faced by a large audience and there was standing room only. Monty's anecdotes were well received, my more sober disquisition on the Liberal approach to welfare treated as a necessary dose of professorial earnestness to be received in quasi-respectful silence, while waiting for the opportunity to have a go at the candidate. It was hot and stuffy in the classroom, and as Willie stood up he pointed to a large burly man propped up against the classroom wall and, speaking like a polished English actor in one of his own plays, said "My man, be so good as to open the window just by your elbow"! "Why doesn't the candidate open the windae himsel'?" burly man shouted. Quick as a flash, Willie countered with "But you know I am a Liberal! I believe in devolution!"

Willie not only failed to be elected but, for the first time, lost his deposit. A second reason for this disappointing result was a complement to the unfortunate failure of his light hearted approach to politics. By coincidence, one of his plays was on a pre-West End tour of the country before its London opening. The major comic character was a Master of Foxhounds who changes his sex! (The actor in question was considered just right for the part—Henry Kendal.) The subject and the associated *mise en scène* was too much for the older ladies of South Edinburgh who, if supposedly of a Liberal disposition, came out, one is told, in droves to vote Tory, or abstained.

When I moved to York I spoke on one or two occasions in support of Richard Rowntree, standing for Parliament in Scarborough. In 1964 on the second of these, after a polished and commendably brief speech by the candidate about our failure to be admitted to the Common Market, a severe looking lady, who reminded me of Auntie Vi, rose to her feet and in stentorian tones maintained that all Liberals should bless General de Gaulle for saying "*non*", he obviously being the instrument of God. The candidate thanked the lady and reminded us that the Liberal Party should always be willing to listen to different opinions. This was too much for the lady, who angrily sprang to her feet shouting "What I have said is not a matter of opinion. It is the REVEALED TRUTH!"

## II: Spreading the Word: Broadcasting

Such experiences helped one's understanding of the political process but could become time-consuming. They could also lead to consideration by the Liberal Party HQ as to one's suitability as a Parliamentary candidate. From the early 1950s the question was put to me several times, and I did not feel tempted. A new temptation presented itself.

Broadcasting contracts of a kind have persisted in being offered me, though nowadays one is only asked for sound bites on current affairs programmes, and I just about manage to persuade broadcasting producers that my time is as valuable as theirs, and that at least they can provide transport to the studio. Early experiences were different. Incursion into broadcasting was brought about not by any positive attempt on my part to use my limited Liberal persona to ask to be heard, but began with invitations from the then Third Programme to speak on professional matters. This was a more satisfactory way of dovetailing my policy interests to my academic obligations.

Indeed, more than this. The Third Programme was regarded increasingly within academic circles as a respectable professional means for disseminating one's ideas, and this included discussion of controversial matters on policy—hence the rather cynical perception of the Third as 'by dons for dons'.[1] It also gave impetus to the necessity of presenting economic ideas in a form in which they were generally understood and considered to be of relevance to the audience, and these requirements applied equally well to attempts to provide economic advice to Liberal, or indeed to any, politicians.

The gradual public realization that the 'crude' version of Keynesianism, which perpetuated the myth that expansion in public expenditure was complementary to the aim of maintaining a high level of employment, was a chimera had a marked effect on the content and structure of broadcasting on public policies. In particular, the 'sermon' type of talk to the proles with some exhortation to be good—a throwback to the Reithian tradition that broadcasting was a public service in which only broadcasters knew what was good for the public who paid for it—could not succeed in peace time. Even if it had continued, there was no longer a consensus, or at least an understanding, that the choice of policies and their relative priority displayed substantial agreement. The BBC's response recognised this in inventing what I call in a Third Programme, donnish way 'the principle of the unidimensional political spectrum'. This was its defence against the frequent charge of being in the pocket of the government in power, and was increasingly invoked in presentation of broadcasted discussions, usually 'live' ones, built round the political cycle of events including, for example,

---

[1] I am sure that there must have been several younger 'dons' like myself who learnt much about clearer presentation of ideas, as well as broadcasting technique, from the producers of programmes claiming a serious intellectual content. I remember in particular, and owe a great debt to, PH Newby (an author of notable distinction), George Bruce (of BBC Scotland, who had been my English teacher at school, and later a very well known poet as well as talks producer), and Steve Banerjee, who coached me for delivery of less recondite talks on economic questions.

the Queen's Speech and the Budget. Discussion was set up to be confrontational with Labour on one side and Tory on the other, with perhaps a guru or two and a Liberal sandwiched in the middle. Many years later, when Chairing the Home Office Committee on the Finance of the BBC (1985–6), I questioned the wisdom of this arrangement as a prime example of 'public service broadcasting' on the grounds that it might be designed to maximize ratings by its entertainment rather than its educational value. Gus (later Lord) Macdonald, then the Chief Executive of STV, was chairing the AGM of the Royal Television Society and upstaged me with a remark which vastly amused the broadcasting audience: 'What Professor Peacock is advocating is that we should all have the courage to be boring!'

Returning to these earlier days of the 1950s and early 1960s, before politicians saw TV as a cardinal element in their growth in public reputation, I had neither the experience nor the professional stature to be considered as a participant in such high-level occasions. Third Programme talks were usually pre-recorded, which meant that revisions could be made before being broadcasted. The next stage towards improvised presentation was to give a 'live' talk on some current economic event from a hastily written script which the producer might only have a few moments to read in advance. I gave a number of these just before I departed for Edinburgh, and on a wide range of issues, usually explaining the background to some proposed change in economic circumstances and policy reactions to it, and over a wide range from why the government was considering abolishing prices imposed on retailers by wholesalers (retail price maintenance) to how the International Monetary Fund works. These were five to eight minutes talks, usually after the Home Service 9 o'clock News. I would be rung up at LSE in the morning with the first intimation on the topic, would write a draft to be picked up by a uniformed BBC official—I'm not sure exactly when but one certainly appeared at the LSE front door wearing white gloves. I would call in at the BBC, go over the script with Steve Banerjee, who was quick to see what needed changing, probably have a glass of wine and a sandwich with him and then wait for the metaphorical starting gun to go off, and, finally, a taxi home. As time went on, I found myself 'promoted' to perform on more auspicious occasions, including three where I talked about the background to the annual budget, once the highlight of the political year, before the political gladiators did battle.

Like all public institutions with a commanding confidence in their mission and in its importance, the BBC had developed a series of rituals owing their origin to a need to set down rules for conduct that took into account the status and function of those who would have to implement them. Fixed in the mists or murk of time these rules may remain in being for long periods, although in the course of time they lose their relevance and potency. For example, it was fascinating working out for oneself the rules governing the effect of the status of the broadcaster on the standard of entertainment offered them. Thus an appearance on *Woman's Hour* (2–3 pm) of ten minutes plus a short question and answer session with the presenter was preceded by a cold lunch of spam and a green salad (with no oil dressing) and perhaps a coffee to follow, the company not necessarily including the presenter who might have better prospects for lunch. (I remember that on one such occasion my solemn talk on the growing 'burden' of state pensions presented by an ageing population was preceded by the much more succulent offering of a recipe for Finnish Liver Pie.) Moving up the hierarchy, which seemed closely correlated with the time of day, water was turned into a respectable wine (in those days a Moselwein) liquefying a buffet supper with ample choice, that is if one were talking about some important issue of the day, and the producer would be expected to entertain one. I liked these occasions for the producers were often highly entertaining, respect for the BBC being coloured by some droll stories about its rituals.

At the top of the list, that I only reached on one occasion, was a dinner served by the BBC butler, whom I remember as a gaunt figure well briefed in the relative status of the participating guests. I was invited because the budget discussion that I was to introduce was to be conducted by no less a guru than the famous economist Roy Harrod. The gastronomic rules clearly indicated that a pre-broadcast dinner was to be ordered and one of the BBC Governors—in those days regarded rather as the High Priests of Culture—felt it necessary to be present, being also a friend of RF himself. When it came to the dinner, I was surprised when the producer, John Brunner, signalled to the butler to serve me first, and I have never found anything in any book of etiquette to suggest that the youngest and least distinguished should receive this honour. (The only thing running through my mind at the time was that perhaps Governors, like medieval princes, employed some lowly creature as a food taster.) The butler brought a plate of smoked salmon to my left—a great delicacy in those days—and I noticed that there were ten pieces on the plate and five guests. I gingerly transferred one piece to my plate and returned the silver serving cutlery. The plate (and the butler) remained anchored on my left. There was silence. Then the butler boomed; "I THINK THAT WE MAY BE ALLOWED TO HAVE ANOTHER PIECE ... *SIR.*" There was nothing I could do to counter this rebuke. I hastily took a further piece—should I have graciously declined the offer with thanks?—and, in true British fashion, the conversation was renewed as if nothing had happened. (Everyone else took two slices!) It would have been hard to anticipate that understanding the conventions of hospitality were part of the qualifications necessary to pursue an anxiety to do good!

# Chapter 9

# The Illusion Persists

### I: The Second Professor Peacock

Although not meant to be a kind of *roman a clef*, I did drop an earlier hint that my brief return to Scotland was not a pronounced success. An attempt had been made to bring me back to occupy the first Professorial appointment in Economics at Dundee but, despite the persuasive powers of Malcolm Knox, to whom I owed so much, now Principal of St Andrews of which Queen's College, Dundee, was still a part, I did not accept. That was in 1954 and I had no intention of leaving LSE or even later in 1956 when I was offered without interview the Chair of Commercial and Political Economy and Mercantile Law (to give it its full title) at Edinburgh.

The circumstances of my leaving London only need explanation here because of their effect on my activities as an active Liberal. Dundee would have produced both professional and personal difficulties. Professionally, the new Department of Economics at Dundee incorporated the staff in Economics from the Dundee School of Economics, a college whose students took the London BSc Degree, several of them older and more experienced than myself. It was unlikely, too, to be a popular appointment amongst the peer group in Scottish Universities, some of whom had offered themselves as candidates for the post. The personal problem was that my father was a senior professor at Dundee, as Professor of Zoology, and I did not have the confidence to believe that I could be insensitive to rumours that nepotism has been employed to have me appointed. I am sure that my father would have been a great support to me, but, although on friendly enough terms with Knox, he was opposed to his policies.

Edinburgh seemed a different proposition. I imagined that I would still be intellectually challenged, would still be in close touch with professional developments at home and abroad, in a place where we as a family would be somewhat better off and with a kinder domestic living environment than the brick-clad semis of North London, good schools close at hand, and in a city which friends and colleagues would like to visit. We also had a personal problem with our eldest child, severely autistic, but Edinburgh medicine and hospital facilities were considered to be in the van of ideas about mental disability.

Had 'anxiety to do good' gone out of the window, now? It might very well have done so, given the preoccupations of moving from an academic establishment where I had few, mostly pleasant, administrative duties and many opportunities to be engaged in professional discussion—a kind of intellectual co-operative—to a largely hierarchical system, not yet under internal challenge, where I was largely individually responsible for the teaching and development of economics. Moreover, one academic skill I had not learnt at LSE, because there it was largely unnecessary, was academic politics and the necessity of being practised in the art of 'rhetoric', much beloved by Scots Professors in persuading colleagues to favour one's viewpoint and to support one's ambitious plans for thwarting those of others. There was much to preoccupy one in settling in.

The test of one's prowess was initially presented in the Professorial Inaugural Lecture in which one laid out to the public a sample of one's academic wares. It was alleged that one had to deliver this lecture within two months of arrival, and only later was I to discover that this was not a rule that had been adhered to within living memory. Taking it seriously meant the sweat of hurried preparation and, remembering the rituals of academic presentation common in Scots universities familiar to me from St. Andrews days, one had to cast aside the informal mannerisms of the seminar. What was demanded was solemn sermon and not cheerful chat.

I rather enjoyed the challenge, and consequently fell into the trap of imagining that what I had to say was of some importance, whether it was to be an introductory lecture to the 450 students in their first year — regarded by older professorial colleagues as *the* major teaching responsibility of holders of a Chair — or a public lecture of some kind. I am not proud of the Inaugural Lecture which was printed in the University Gazette, and have lived to regret offering the *obiter dictum* that 'one does not emulate the work of Adam Smith simply by being an authority on what he had written' — may Historians of Economic Thought forgive me!

But the relevance of this new-found challenge went deeper. Although I fought to keep abreast with developments in my own specialism, there is no doubt that I spent far too much time trying to act the role of the imparter of economic wisdom — and still being under 40 years of age, too! I should have taken more seriously the student who — it being a brave thing to do in those days — wrote reviews of the lecturing performance of professors in the student magazine. He described my lectures as 'quirky' and, in retrospect, I believe that to be correct. But the main point is that as lectures were usually based on a prepared text, a theatrical presentation is what it became; and such an occasion began to affect one's writing. In my case, pedantry and pomposity are still charges which stick in describing my writing, whatever attempts are made to eliminate them.

## II: *Also Sprach Der Professor*

It was my continuing interest in advising the Liberal Party which put this to the test. Three years or so after taking up my post in Edinburgh, I was asked to give a lecture at the Liberal Summer School to be held in Girton College, Cambridge, in July 1960.

The Summer School had an interesting history. It was largely the brainchild of Ramsay Muir, once extremely well known as a liberal thinker and activist during the 1920s and

30s. He had the support of Ernest Simon and Walter Layton, editor of the Economist (whom I met many years afterwards), but what particularly interested me was that his co-founders included Maynard Keynes and Hubert Henderson, the latter once being one of the best known academic economists in my trade. The School was an arm of Muir's efforts to promulgate contemporary ideas that might be embodied in Liberal policies, notably in reconciling the need to preserve competition both nationally and internationally whilst developing a compatible social policy. In 1931 Keynes himself had delivered one of his most famous inter-war utterances on policy at the School entitled 'The End of Laissez-Faire'. (Muir had paved the way for the preparation of the famous Yellow Book mentioned in Chapter 7.)[1]

Of course, I was delighted and accepted. I could see this as an opportunity to develop some of the ideas in my piece for *The Unservile State*, fortified by some notes I had prepared for a lecture on liberalist thought and the future of liberalism delivered at the University of Virginia in the autumn of 1958.[2] There were three strands to this attempt to interest a critical Liberal audience in new ideas on social policy, and one which still kept before one a continuing emphasis on personal freedom and the responsibilities associated with its exercise.

The first strand was that of having as clear an idea as possible of the liberal ethic on the distribution of wealth,

---

[1]    I owe this short account from information supplied by the Liberal Democrat History Group, which includes a biography of Ramsay Muir prepared by Richard Grayson, Director of Policy of the Liberal Democrats. I am grateful to the Group and to Mr Grayson for this.

[2]    At the invitation of James Buchanan, then Professor of Economics there, to become one of the best known philosophers of economic thought, awarded the Nobel Prize in Economics in 1986. We shared an interest in the economics of government built round our mutual admiration of earlier Italian writers. He prepared some excellent translations from the Italian for my jointly edited work with Richard Musgrave, *Classics in the Theory of Public Finance* (1958), still in print. 'Jim' was not entirely pleased with my lecture, mainly because he thought, like several of his US peers, that I was 'soft' on J.M. Keynes', still mistakenly regarded as a dangerous socialist. However, we have remained friends.

including both income and capital. It is always a problem that this prime element in the achievement of a free society can lead to continual dispute even amongst liberals themselves, although those of this persuasion are not alone alongside socialists who have bitter controversies of their own about income distribution.

There is a formidable professional literature in economics devoted to the finer points of the philosophy of distribution and how any particular philosophy may be turned into a set of policy measures that governments can introduce, the overriding condition in a democracy being acceptability. It would try the reader's patience to indulge in a disquisition on this matter and to emerge from the labyrinthine journey through the philosophical maze with some liberal policy set in tablets of stone. What is done below is to show how my thoughts on distribution developed since the publication of *The Welfare Society*.

It followed that the first consideration was to define a target for a satisfactory income distribution. The overriding concern for liberals was, as Beveridge had already emphasized, to abolish poverty, if need be by some form of collective action. It has already been shown that meeting even the most austere definition of where the poverty line should be drawn, required some form of positive redistribution, unless in the course of economic progress the income distribution would automatically adjust so that the there would be no necessity for public intervention. The pre-conditions for this last proviso to become operative seemed unlikely to emerge. In any case, as already observed, growth in prosperity can have a marked effect on public perceptions of how poverty is defined. (There came point where it was said that the dividing line separated off the poor as those who could not afford a colour TV.) It must be noted that there was a cardinal difference here between a liberal view on *minimum* income 'needs' and the left wing view that the object of state intervention should be much more radical, offering support for *uniformity* in income levels and even an equal income distribution.

Of course, in an ideal world, the aim of removing poverty was more satisfactorily achieved from a liberal point of view if it did not require government intervention at all, or only some very limited degree of intervention. There seemed little immediate prospect of that, but that defined an important responsibility for government, so far as liberal philosophy was concerned, namely positive intervention in order to reduce the degree of intervention itself.

This formed the second strand of one's perception of policy which could be differentiated from socialist measures. Whatever doubt I had about the necessity for an elaborate national insurance scheme, one must pay tribute to Beveridge for recognizing this important point which he associated with the pre-conditions of the scheme itself. It would require government intervention to improve the access of education and health, including suitable housing, by the poor and disadvantaged (such as those born with a disability of some kind). It would be unfair to criticize Beveridge for not working out in detail how such intervention should be carried through, although for the rest of his life he lamented the Labour Government's methods of reliance on centralised nationalised services, coupled with finance largely raised through general taxation (see reference to his speech to the Royal Economic Society, above, Chapter 7).

Trying to do so was not an easy matter, and, even if it could be instituted along the lines I suggested, the proposed methods by their very unfamiliarity, would encounter political opposition. I outline them in more detail below, but their essential components were to provide financial support for access to health, education and housing, to individuals, leaving it open for a system of provision that need not be confined to publicly operated concerns, ie state schools, hospitals and housing authorities, that would encourage the availability of alternative sources of supply to beneficiaries and reduce the costs of entry to provision of such services as a way of keeping incumbent producers on their toes.

There is a further matter concerning the general argument for an approach of this kind to a welfare society. Obviously such an approach supports a move towards giving individuals more freedom of choice over important aspects of their lives and which would enable them to gain an understanding of and more control over their long-run aims and aspirations, and how to allow for the many uncertainties of life. Whereas that second strand concentrated on what nowadays is called 'investment in human capital', this third strand considered the question of the distribution of physical capital either in the form of personally owned property or financial claims on it. The inequality in the distribution of capital and particularly of land was a major concern of Liberal political philosophers prior to the early 20th-century welfare reforms introduced by the Liberal administration. It had wide political and economic implications. Given the acceptance of a property qualification for becoming a voter in Parliamentary and local elections, it could result in disenfranchisement of the poor which in itself would reduce their influence on the economic decisions of government. With a large proportion of property acquired by inheritance, there was no guarantee that capital resources would be used as productively as previous generations had done and who had accumulated them. The rate of growth in output and in the demand for labour were likely to diminish. The great liberal exponent of this position was, of course, John Stuart Mill,[3] who explored in detail how the laws of inheritance and the taxation of inheritance should reflect the aspirations of a liberal society.

The reader will find that I have funked an analysis of the relation between the distribution of wealth and welfare state policies, other than to acknowledge that the content of the latter could depend on the view taken of the former. The

[3]   See J.S. Mill, *Principles of Political Economy* Vol. 2, ed. VW Bladen and JM Robson, University of Toronto Press edition, 1965, Book III Chapter IX sections 1–4. The first edition of this famous work first appeared in 1848, the same year as the Marx/Engels *Communist Manifesto*. Mill also considers in detail other important aspects of the distribution of wealth, notably in regard to the rights of women, schemes for co-ownership of businesses, and capital ownership by government. I was pleasantly surprised when, in a recent polling of readers of *Liberal History Review*, on who was the greatest ever liberal thinker and activist, John Stuart Mill headed all the rest

philosophical issues, as is clear in Mill, are difficult to unravel, and, whatever principles were derived from them, their translation into policy measures rested on a knowledge of both economics and law that I did not then possess. There was a good practical reason for stopping short of entering this minefield of speculation. I was not asked to give a course of academic lectures, as the subject required, but an exposition closely related to the current concerns of Party members and sympathizers. I give it only passing mention.

Nevertheless, doubts about the distribution of wealth that is the outcome of a largely uncontrolled economy suggest some affinity with socialist ideas. That this is not so became apparent in the post WW1 period, when the views of prominent Socialist thinkers, who were also activists, are considered. Notable amongst them were Hugh Dalton and Barbara Wootton, both of whom were members of the Colwyn Committee on National Debt and Taxation which reported in 1927.[4] Dalton sought to develop a scheme that would favour the forced sale of inheritable property to the government, who would then decide whether to add it to the state's capital assets or whether to sell inherited property on, with the prospect of using the proceeds to reduce the size of the national debt, itself, he believed, mainly in the hands of the rich. Like his teacher, Arthur Cecil Pigou, once as famous as Keynes (who also had earlier been one Pigou's students), Dalton saw much in favour of the scheme invented by the Italian socialist writer, Rignano, that inher-

---

[4]    The Colwyn Committee was set up by the then Chancellor of the Exchequer, Winston Churchill, mainly to investigate methods for reducing the size of the national debt that had grown to what would then be regarded as alarming proportions, mainly as a result of the financing of WW1. I started to study the taxation of inheritance on my promotion to Reader at LSE in 1951 and, apart from a short article on the taxation of wealth published in 1965, it was 2002, i.e. half a century later, that I wrote up some of the research! Only specialists are likely to have an interest in the result — see Alan Peacock and Ilde Rizzo, 'The Diffusion of Economic Ideas: The Rignano Example', *Revista di Diritto Finanziario e Sciencza delleFinanze*, 2002, Volume 4, pp. 547–74. The article includes an analysis of Dalton's perception of the 'desirable' ways of taxing inheritance.

ited property should be taxed progressively through time. In broad terms, this meant taxing it by a modest percentage of its value on its first transfer, a higher percentage on the second, and at a rate of 100 per cent on the third.

Dalton introduced a variant of the Rignano scheme by which at the third transfer the donee would be compensated by the issue of terminable annuities. The scheme received a good run for its money by the Colwyn Committee, but it requires little imagination to list the practical difficulties that such a scheme would encounter. (Not surprisingly, the Inland Revenue [cf. Chapter 4 above], were able to produce some formidable administrative obstacles to the Rignano approach, not to speak of their scepticism, shared by several contemporary economists, about the disincentive effects of such a capital taxation regime.)

One might have been tempted by considering the possibility of producing a version of Rignano more in accordance with a liberal economic and social policy, a kind of counterpart to the earlier attempts to amalgamate income tax and social security coupled with negative taxation. However, that would obscure the main aim of any liberal scheme of capital distribution — to produce greater equality in the distribution of wealth for the purpose of giving individuals the opportunity and the means to investment according to their own assessment of their welfare. The very opportunity can frequently result in the rapid accumulation of wealth by an individual through his/her own efforts and this should not be discouraged, particularly if these efforts improved the opportunities of others through their affects on any growth in incomes and employment. Rignano's scheme recognized this in reducing discouragement to accumulation by low taxation of the first transfer of property through inheritance, and few Classical economists would have disagreed with him about the lack of incentives to future generations of donees to act in the public interest when access to capital did not depend on their own efforts. However, that was not his sole objective.

It is here that John Stuart Mill points the way forward, but Rignano's admiration for JSM did not extend to following the latter's recommended route. A tax on the size of the estate passing at death takes no account of the circumstances of the donee who might be anywhere in the income or wealth scale. It would be purely random in its effect on the distribution of wealth for the whole community. He proposed that the size of the tax should depend on the *circumstances of the donee*, such that the lower a donee down the wealth scale, the lower the amount of tax paid. Given a propensity of taxpayers to minimize the amount of tax payable to the state, then this objective is best achieved by the donor transferring wealth passing at death to the poorer potential beneficiaries.

Mill's proposal is an excellent example of an attempt, as he would have called it, to 'outline the social philosophy to which political economy might lead', a somewhat unfashionable activity today when devising methods for implementing political proposals that have a firm analytical base requires skills that seem to take up too much time to acquire in the process of making a living, and that may brand you as a political zealot rather than as a cautious scientist.

Certainly, it is not self-evident from economic analysis that the scheme would produce the desired result which would depend on such complications as the disposition of the donor to the various donees, as well as the incentive effects on the donor him or herself. Nor would the legal and administrative problems of implementation seem any the less formidable than those encountered in a straightforward tax on total sum passing at death.

While the prospect of examining a form of wealth redistribution of particular appeal to liberals was inviting, there was little prospect of offering a scheme that might stand up to public scrutiny, and in a matter of a few weeks when the Summer School Lecture was due to be delivered. As it is, after an analysis of the state of the British economy and the prospects for government expenditure of the kind set out in the discussion in 1955 with Beveridge, Chambers and Clark (See Chapter 7, Annex), painting a somewhat optimistic picture of the future of the British economy, I offer a comment on a set of reforms that would bring welfare policy into line with liberal thinking. Actually, they seem rather mild and presented in a pussyfooted manner, alongside their descendants put forward in the 1980s (see the appropriate excerpt from the published version of the lecture which appears in Annex 9.1 to this Chapter.) The lecture was well received but I might have been deluded in believing this because the predominantly female audience were a model of politeness.

Press reports (e.g. *Guardian*,. August 1, 1960), seemed to regard the proposals for change as preaching *laissez-faire* by implication taking a reactionary rather than a radical stance on social policy. Younger liberal academics were very sensitive about being branded in this way, and I felt obliged to write to the friendly *Guardian* denying that I should be tarred by this offensive brush. This is what I wrote:

> Sir—I appreciate the difficulties facing your reporter in condensing the substance of my address to the Liberal Summer School last Saturday in order to fit the available space, but this account might give the impression that I was preaching an extreme form of laissez-faire.
>
> I did express concern at the likely continuance of the present proportion of Government expenditure to national income, but I criticised in no uncertain terms those who would have us believe that the present absolute level of Government expenditure should be pegged or even reduced. Indeed, I suggested that some forms of Government expenditure, for example road development, might be increased rapidly.
>
> I did express the wish that certain parts of the edifice of the Welfare State should be dismantled, but only when we could be sure that the large majority of the working population would be in a position to save for their future needs. I did criticise the impending introduction of the differential national pensions scheme, but at the same time supported the payment of an increased flat-rate retirement pension immediately, which would be payable as of right and subject to no earnings limit.
>
> I did propose the gradual extension of charging for some social services according to individual benefit, but I recognised the existence of benefits to the community in these services which should continue to be met out of general taxation.
>
> In short, I was suggesting how we might move towards a position where individuals would wish to rely less and less on the State for the provision of needs which they could

meet themselves, given a continuing rise in our prosperity which would be widely distributed. I hoped to prove wrong Processor Hayek and others of his way of thinking who assert that the Welfare State is and will continue to be a threat to our liberty. — Yours etc

   Alan T Peacock, Professor of Economic Science, University of Edinburgh (*The Guardian*, 4 August 1960, p. 6).

The letter was written at speed and, as is commonly the case, one regrets not having taken the time to produce a more balanced view of what one had intended to say. With the benefit of hindsight, I see two faults in it when considered against the background of my gropings towards a coherent liberal economic philosophy.

This was the move towards the privatization of housing, which I disguise in the lecture as a new initiative to be taken by local governments. In fact, the principle behind this proposal would require local authorities to be deprived of the power to determine the conditions of sale, notably by measures that would still have allowed them to rig the market through the bidding process and the favouring of particular classes of bidders. I had failed to make the useful political point that freeing the housing market would be an effective way of reducing the power of local authorities dominated by one party, whose control over housing to rent could be and had been used as a vote-rigging device.

Journalists looking for a slogan found one in the lecture. I thought it rather effective at the time but now it makes me blush with shame. It appears at the bottom of p. 11 of the text in the only sentence in it which is italicized: '*the true object of the welfare state is to teach people how to do without it*'. This falls into that well-worn category of 'things that might have been better expressed'. Surely I meant 'persuade people to do without it' or 'the true function of the welfare state is to create the circumstances which render it unnecessary'. However, I was lumbered with the original which, when quoted with approval by Nigel Nicolson MP in some debate in the House of Commons, was greeted with a torrent of laughter. It has appeared, so it seems, on more than one occasion as a degree examination question with the word 'Discuss' following the quote. I have never waited to hear what the answers were like!

The paternalistic flavour of the 'slogan' seemed to indicate that I had been head of an essentially hierarchical university department too long, not sufficiently challenged professionally, rapidly becoming infected with *folie de grandeur*, and insufficiently trained in political skills. It was time to move on.

**Annex 9.1:  Extract from *The Welfare Society* (Unservile State Papers No 2), pp. 6–8**

*Liberal Attitudes*

We can hardly claim that Liberals are united today on the issue of public expenditure. There are those who seem to seek inspiration in the Gladstonian tradition of the 'saving of candle ends', and there are those who see in the Welfare State the fulfilment of the aims of the famous Liberal Government of the early years of this century. Who is right?

There is nothing surprising, nothing wrong, and nothing intellectually disreputable in this disagreement. It does not represent a failure to comprehend some important 'scientific' principle which we must accept because it rests on 'expert' knowledge of what our society needs. In a technocratic world, one might be bamboozled into believing that there is some 'correct' percentage of national income which should be devoted to particular kinds of service and which can be derived from 'scientific' principles. Such is the idea that the 'correct' amount to be spent on state education is round about 5 per cent of the national income. This is nonsense. The evaluation of educational or any other service cannot be based on some supposedly objective indicator like the number of children per class. If we increase our expenditure on education, it must be because we consider this increase is better spent on education *than other things*. Or, as the economist would put it, the increased cost of education is valued in terms of the alternatives we have to forego, including not only other forms of government expenditure but also the increased taxes we would otherwise not have to pay. In a democracy, therefore, the evaluation of the different services of government depends, ultimately at least, on those who pay the taxes and we have no scientific means of evaluating the taxpayers' choices. All that the educationist, the health, the housing, and the town planning expert can do for us is to tell us what can be achieved with differing amounts of expenditure. But the experts have no right to make the ultimate choices about the amounts of expenditure on individual services because no person has a monopoly of values. We may be influenced by their personal judgments, but we cannot let them dictate to us. To think otherwise is to accept paternalistic government.

There are those, even among those who regard themselves as radical liberals, who believe that the democratic process does not lead to a 'correct' appraisal of the rôle of government in society. The most notable exponent of this view is Professor Kenneth Galbraith who, in his influential work *The Affluent Society* (1958), has made even drawing-room conversation on public finance possible by the invention of some colourful catch-phrases. The most obvious task of an affluent society, in his view, is to redress the 'imbalance' between public and private expenditure in favour of the former. This is necessary because of three important factors. The first is one which we have noted in passing — the complementarity between private and public consumption as represented in the common example of the increased use of cars and the need for improved roads. The second is that 'consumer sovereignty' is a myth in a world of persuasive advertising, and that the benefits of public expenditure are underestimated because they cannot be advertised — 'a politician or public servant who dreams up a new public service is a wastrel' (p. 261). Yet the kinds of educational and cultural activities which represent the peak of achievement in our civilisation require, according to Galbraith, vigorous action by the Government by way of better schools and public amenities. Thirdly, the custodians of the 'conventional wisdom' — the heads of large business and financial corporations — see in the growth of the public sector a threat to efficiency and enterprise. They are worshippers before the idol of Economic Growth but if increasing production simply means that more people die of too much food than too little, clothing becomes plumage rather than protection, and cars decorative chariots rather than means of transport, then it is absurd (says Galbraith) to make a fetish of production.

Within the context of the American scene, there is much that is persuasive about Galbraith's argument, and his

appeal for bigger and better government is to the reader's
sense of values as much as to any technical facts about the
performance of government. What is surprising is that anyone should imagine that it has any immediate relevance to
the British scene. The crucial point is that the Federal Government in the United States spends an amount equal to
about 15 per cent of the Gross National Product (National
Income), while in the United Kingdom the figure for
Central Government alone is 27 per cent. It is true that a
federal structure of government means that local finance
plays a more important rôle, but even if we compare all
government expenditure with national income, the figure
in the United States is about 24 per cent compared with
about 35 per cent in the United Kingdom. As a nation we
need little persuading on the merits of government expenditure. Indeed, the custodians of 'conventional wisdom' in
Britain may be said to be those who unquestioningly
assume that any new social or economic problem requires a
new government department.

Chapter 10

# *Liberal Political Philosophy and Public Action*

In the course of pursuing further the place of Ramsay Muir in his attempts to bring liberal political philosophy to bear on policy, one finds that he had acquired a reputation for putting barriers in the way of reform. In the *Oxford Dictionary of National Biography* he is regarded by his biographer, David Cregier, as a major but not outstanding figure in Liberal Party history. Cregier is in obvious sympathy with the judgement, as he put it, that Muir 'was accused of a regression from the radical social democratic liberalism of 'New Liberalism' of the early 1900s to a more traditional, individualistic, Liberalism' (see *Dictionary of National Biography*, Oxford, 2004, Vol. 39, pp. 669–670) It is questionable whether traditional Liberalism was so firmly based on individualism in the 19th century as implied in the statement, although there was a strong emphasis on the commercial aspects of Liberal policy, such as Free Trade, that appealed to Northern business interests, particularly in Manchester. However, while that is a relevant issue in any discussion of the origins of Liberal party policies, the interesting thing about Cregier's judgement on Muir is that it is assumed that the impregnation of Liberal party policies with a dose of 'social democracy' was a firm step in the right direction in the evolution of liberal political philosophy. The 'Welsh passion' behind the establishment of the welfare state, now a

century old, simply accepted that concern for the rapid
improvement of social services must require a large extension in government intervention. Moreover, the form of
intervention need not be confined to transfers of income to
individuals but must also be extended to educational institutions directly, such as universities who were thereby able
to abolish fees. Even this was not going far enough, for the
*provision* of the major part of schooling was to lie with gov-
ernment-owned institutions where teachers and other staff
became national government or local government employees. Finally, that important pre-condition for the operation
of a 'viable' pensions system, namely a national health
service, was perceived by Beveridge as well as by 'radical'
enthusiasts as an integral part of a Liberal welfare policy,
though there might be differences in emphasis over
whether a national health service should charge for its
services, paid for from individual health insurance policies,
themselves receiving some funding from state sources as
a way of producing some equalization of individual
contributions.

It was no accident, therefore, that the electorate subjected
to the Labour Party version of a welfare state as introduced
in 1948, would be confused about the question as to what
was the difference between its version and that of the Liberal Party, other, perhaps, than the latter's usefulness as a
vehicle for channelling complaints about how it actually
worked and over some of its more ludicrous arrangements,
such as penalizing pensioners who worked after official
retirement. It is doubly confusing when it is claimed, even
today, that the Labour Party were the true founders of what
are essentially 'social democratic' views on social policy.[1]

My move to York coincided with a decision to re-examine
the liberal principles that should determine the shape and
content of Liberal social policy, but having regard to how
these principles covered the whole spectrum of policy and
therefore how policies were to be reconciled with one

---

[1]   For a most original and striking discussion of this issue, see the final
      essay in George Watson's *Take Back the Past: Myths of the Twentieth
      Century*, The Lutterworth Press, 2007.

another, and how their implementation took account of economic realities. At least that was the general idea.

This meant searching out for any complementarities with my overriding obligation to a completely new university in which I had been appointed, and willingly accepted. The remit was to set up the social sciences, recruit staff and students, institute graduate studies in economics and encourage research, and was recognized by appointment at the top rate payable to a 'non-medical, non clinical' Professor of £3,300 per annum (1962).

Much might be said about this 'translation' to York from Edinburgh, but this account only mentions those circumstances affecting attempts to influence Liberal Party policy and then only up to 1967. Briefly put, progress was made in my understanding of liberalism where the search for 'complementarity' was successful because of the opportunity of talking through such matters with (mostly) fellow economists and crossing swords with others at least disposed to have a friendly go at me, and with whom I remained on amicable terms throughout my professional life. Much to my surprise, I find that my views came more into sympathy with Muir's position, though I had doubts about his policy proposals. That, I suppose, is what landed me in trouble.

I write this at a time (March 2009) of fierce discussion about policies designed to cope with our current economic difficulties. If one judged from press reports and economic punditry, we are undergoing a traumatic economic situation comparable with the Great Depression of the early 1930s and with similar auguries of impending disaster with falling real incomes and rising unemployment, all overshadowed by countries undergoing the same experience or in a position, so it seems, to be at the mercy of oil-producing nations who include unfriendly governments. Additionally, our governments are obsessed by the problem of climate change and seem determined to introduce long-term measures that would entail widespread intervention in the day-to-day lives of ordinary citizens.[2]

In such circumstances, devoting one's residual intellectual energies at a great age to what appear to be the minutiae of social policy and to offer policy proposals for the long-term seems almost a frivolous pursuit. However, the usual solutions to economic crises have frequently been associated with growing government participation in the provision of goods and services through nationalisation, growing use of the tax system to restrict private spending, and growing regulation of economic transactions between private persons and businesses. The rest of my attempts to relieve my 'anxiety to good' may be worth the telling because it led directly to a later attempt to disassociate liberalism from a growing need to achieve its aims by more public action instead of by other means, or at least to drastically alter its form. Of course, it was something of a joke to assume that the supply of any ideas I had would follow the so-called law of the economist Jean Baptiste Say that 'supply would create its own demand'.

I failed in the attempt to convince even a small minority party, the then Liberals, that these policies had substance, not only because I overestimated any influence I might have to convince them that these were worth serious consideration, but, more directly important to me, because I now appeared not to have paid sufficient attention to a lesson to be learnt from my own professional discipline. The difficulty is encapsulated in the distinction between a static and dynamic approach to policy problems. I gain little consolation from the fact that it is a distinction that sometimes still goes unrecognized in discussion of policy problems by highly skilled and influential economists, even to this day. Economic modelling of public policy tends to be in 'comparative static' form. For example, an existing economic situation, considered politically to be in some sense unsatis-

---

[2]    That the basis of these policies is highly questionable is argued in Colin Robinson (editor and contributor), *Climate Change Policy*, IEA, 2008. My own contribution is devoted to the issues of how these policies impinge on individual freedom.

factory is compared to an alternative situation which takes account of policy changes based on economic analysis which are designed to improve that situation. However, this mechanical view of a policy change does not take account of the *process* by which this change is introduced. Or in more colloquial terms, the model specifies the goal of the change but does not properly identify the path to reach it. I have known economists who would argue very strongly that this process is beyond the reach of economic analysis and is the job of administrators to sort out. However, the economist can have useful things to say is about the 'feed back' that is likely to occur as the result of an attempt to implement the policy change. This may be difficult to forecast and to forestall, but the recent extension of economic analysis to cover the study of the behaviour of bureaucracies and the reactions of public and their pressure groups to bureaucratic action has much to offer. The proposed reforms that were to be scuppered by the Liberal Party high-level activists did not entirely lack attention to the 'costs of implementation' of these proposals, but they were not fully worked out.

The missing piece in the jigsaw of social policy, in my view, was what to do in order to redress the balance of advantage lying with those who attained (or retained) a position of relative affluence by access to capital as compared to those without such access. Contemporary economic thought in the 1960s put increasing emphasis on the role of investment in human capital as a major factor in explaining relative economic growth, with access to education as its principal component. Of course, Liberals in particular had always maintained that their concept of what they termed 'social justice' included such access, and that expansion of elementary and secondary education was simply the right of all and required government support for poorer families. An educated citizenry was seen as a pre-condition for the operation of a political system where the consent of the governed was a necessary condition of operation. But the principle of access did not clearly define the boundaries of policy, and a desire to maintain and improve material prosperity readily suggested that educational rights extended to access to higher education.

One can readily imagine how politicians could take such an antiseptic statement of the case for a wide expansion of education and turn it into the colourful language that would impress voters upon whom their continuation in office depends. Examples are legion. Liberal activists might favour an approach designed to solve four problems:

i)   *The Politico-Philosophical Problem*
     Defining the extent of the political commitment to expansion and the general position of government to assume responsibility for meeting this commitment.

ii)  *The Organisational Problem*
     The respective roles of central and local governments and of private institutions in meeting the commitment.

iii) *The Educational Problem*
     The extent to which government(s) should 'steer' the education system in order to encourage some lines of study and practice rather than to allow students to decide on where their talents and interests lay as a guide to their choices.

iv)  *The Resources Problem*
     This is colloquially thought of as essentially a financial question. How far government(s) should provide the finance in the form of loans and grants etc to educational institutions rather than to expect them to raise finance themselves helped by tax relief. Likewise, the extent to which financial support should be principally given to customers, ie students, in the form of grants and loans and the conditions to be attached to them. In turn, what were the implications for government methods of financing resources, given its power to tax and raise loans?

It is all too easy to fall into this way of thinking that somehow a master plan implemented by government is a precondition for finding the 'correct' solution to a social problem. Indeed, the above layout of the problems of policy would fit uncomfortably closely to the way thinking on investment in human capital developed during the 1960s when it reached the forefront of policy discussion. Two warning signals derived from a liberal political philosophy need to be launched before the narrative on the anxiety to do good can be resumed.

The first is that the libertarian basis of liberal philosophy is to be found in leaving to the individual the important choices that affect the passage through life, and this includes the right to choose the education that best fits with the individual's perception of what is best for him/her. This clearly does not preclude the taking of advice about such choices, where and what to study and what 'costs' are likely to be associated with such choices. This presupposes that individuals are of sufficient maturity, percipience and incentive to know how to obtain such advice, which clearly can only be assumed when they become adults. Such choices have to be made in their interests by parents and guardians.

The state's role cannot be precisely derived from such a generalized view of liberal political philosophy. However, one can envisage liberal support for measures to ensure that the educational standards are maintained, and that parents and students are served with accurate information about the choices of subjects studied and of the educational institutions offering their services. Extending its function to the specification of target numbers for different subjects of study at school or university, and to the actual provision of education through centralized state institutions with prescribed staff/student ratios, uniform pay scales for staff and financed wholly from taxes, goes far beyond the liberal remit. It is to be noted that this approach not only restricts individual choice but moves towards the suppression of all competition.

This negative opinion of educational central planning is often criticized as favouring the rich and well informed, but this criticism is far from complete, and, I fear, its supporters include those who do not want to complete it. There is nothing in making individual choice the bedrock of liberal political philosophy that precludes extending the previous policies regarding income support to the funding of education, but in the form of payments to the student or pupil to cover at least the direct costs of their education.

The second warning signal to those who countered the growing emphasis on state control by reference to the fundamentals of liberal political philosophy as the starting point for devising policy lies in the adjustments that would be necessary in the existing provision of educational services. Here one returns to the question as to whether the economist has anything useful to say about how one could time such adjustments constrained by the likelihood of gaining their acceptance. The pre-requisite for doing so would be to convince public officials whose power lay in the total grasp that they claimed to have of the feasibility of administrative changes and the democratic decision making process as then currently in place.

Consider the then existing system of education. In the 1960s, something like nine-tenths of the pupils were in local authority schools with their education financed entirely from public funding, a large part of it provided by central government. The remaining privately educated pupils in independent grammar schools and public schools were financed by fees and scholarships, though such schools had tax privileges if they had charitable status. The independent sector had close relations with Oxford and Cambridge through tied scholarships and long-established contacts through former pupils who had become dons and senior civil servants. The ideological war of the period was concentrated on the elitist nature of the independent sector and the economic as well as social advantages that enabled their pupils and students to be appointed to the top jobs in government and the professions. The poor with a state education had to overcome the barriers of what were perceived as a lower standard of attainment and the risks attached to making a long-term decision to go to university when the opportunity cost of going there instead of straight into a job after schooling might be too high. Although the post-war period had seen the expansion of higher education facilities, the abolition of university fees on a considerable scale and the availability of student grants towards tuition and living costs, yet these measures did not seem adequate to achieve more equitable treatment as prescribed by 'social justice' and to increase the pace of investment in human capital to maintain and improve material prosperity, both widely accepted political objectives.[3]

The attempt to stem the tide of collectivist advance in educational policy, aspects of which clearly appealed to influential Liberal activists, appears in retrospect as having been doomed to failure. It did not seem like this at the time, particularly as the proposals that I put forward received strong support from other like-minded liberals. The gap between the logic of the economics of social policy from a liberal standpoint and what the First Marquis of Halifax labelled the 'rough trade' of politics proved to be too great. Now for the story of how an anxiety to do good went from a high expectation of fulfilment to manifest failure.

---

[3]  Of course, this is a very superficial account of the social history of education of the period. However, it is enough to fulfil the purpose of highlighting the contrast between liberal policy aspirations as I saw them, and the gap between these and the policies currently in operation. The reader will obtain a most enlightening account of the impact of educational policy of the time on liberal political thinking in Jo Grimond, *The Liberal Challenge*, Hollis and Carter, 1963, Chapter VII on Education.

# Chapter 11

# Entanglement in the Education Debate

## I: Identifying a Liberal Policy

Alongside the stimulus of debate amongst academic economists at York and London, two people are important in the subsequent saga of my trying to engineer change in liberal thinking regarding the economics of social policy — Jo Grimond and Jack Wiseman — and particularly in defining the goals of educational policy.

It would be an impertinence for me to provide a pen picture of Jo's career and catalogue of abilities, given the available documentation. What needs saying is, alongside taking part in the growing number of Parliamentary debates and committees on educational matters alone in the 1960s, he had developed firm views of his own (see J Grimond, *op. cit.*, cf/fn — Chapter 10).

One has to bear in mind that he was writing at a time when the Liberal Party advisers on educational policy followed the long-established path of educationists mostly taken up with a philosophical exegesis on its function. This was to be derived from the fundamental proposition that education is designed to offer instruction to those chosen to undergo its disciplines and thereby turned out as high-minded, clear-thinking and altruistic beings who would set an example to those less fortunate than themselves.

There was a distinct liberal flavour introduced into this traditional concern of educationists that turned it into a quite formidable radical political force. The first element was to more clearly delineate the definition of the 'chosen'. Hence the battle led by John Stuart Mill, not forgetting his formidable partner Harriet Taylor, to include women in the category of the 'chosen', to remove all religious qualification to access to universities so opening the doors — already wide open in Scotland, one must add — which was a potent force in the 'battle' to chip away at the Oxbridge duopoly. The second element was to facilitate entry into secondary and higher education for those who lacked the means to finance their education, thus lowering the opportunity cost represented by having to leave school in order to work for a living.

What was once a struggle in which liberalism led the way in the political implementation of the basic requirements to meet the radical point of view, is now largely beyond dispute. Liberal educationists imbued with the basic philosophy, at least up to the time covered in this volume, turned their minds to the content of the curriculum, to pedagogic methods and the administrative organisation of educational provision. (What this meant to liberal educationists of the time is carefully argued in John Armitage's essay in *The Unservile State*, Chapter VII.)

This is not quite true. There is some evidence that they realised that the limitations to any utopian schemes were set by the many alternative claims on the public purse. Even so, the fact remains that someone such as ADC Peterson, Professor of Education at Oxford and then Chairman of the Liberal Party Committee on Education, whether or not he was aware of these limitations, nevertheless saw education as primarily the responsibility of the State. This attitude was guided no doubt, in principle at least, by public opinion through the political process and therefore was not simply the outcome of individual aspirations, intellectual qualities and concentrated study, but included freedom of choice in what and where to study and which profession or calling to pursue. It is not necessary to suppose that the disparate views of educationists and economists may be traced to these differences in the philosophy of education and of the content of educational policy. The differences lie more in the perceptions of specialists in the methods of public intervention in educational provision and particularly those relating to financial support to spread its benefits. This proves to be of more fundamental importance in liberal political thinking and action than appears at first sight.

Jo Grimond was thoroughly familiar with contemporary views on educational policy. In the aforementioned Chapter 10 he quotes Peterson with approval in regard to liberal aims:

> Politics means priorities. As a nation we have great but limited resources. The question we have to decide is what comes first, where we shall make or maim investment. I believe that the investment should be made in people ... Liberals have always believed that people count. The best investment that we can make is a free, educated and skilful generation to succeed us. (*A Liberal Design for Education*, Liberal Publication Department)

Jo took this as the starting point of his own commentary on both the organisation and content of educational provision which provided several political glosses on some of Peterson's ideas. For example, he was much in favour of reducing the role of the central government, confining its function to the surveillance of standards of provision and to rectifying the lack of educational research, and to the devolution of administration and provision of educational services to local authorities, but with the full realisation that this could only take place within the Liberals' proposals for devolution of government generally, then, of course, unrealisable.

It is only necessary to give some general idea of the thrust of Jo's approach to educational provision. What is more important is that he was aware of a big gap in Peterson's general argument without actually having to say so! Education may be a fundamental individual right procured through social investment, but this does not exempt it from being weighed against other so-called social investments supplied from public funding.

Up to a certain age it is probably best to forget about too nice a calculation on the worth of education. But after a

certain stage there is a case for applying to this social investment some of the criteria we apply to other economic activities (*op. cit.*, p. 179).

In short Jo recognized the opportunity cost problem that
besets all public expenditure and, indeed, private expenditure decisions. He then adds:

> Let me say in passing that much of the instinctive reaction
> against the type of scrutiny which Professor Peacock (*Pub-
> lic Expenditure: Appraisal and Control*, Alan T. Peacock and
> Others, Oliver and Boyd, 1963) has applied to education …
> is the result of treating economics as a mathematical subject
> divorced from value judgments, and also the result of the
> refusal to apply logical examination where it may seem to
> cut across the sentimental assumptions of a wholly unreal
> scale of values (*op. cit.*, pp. 179–80).

This passage has been singled out, not because it suggests
that I had, at the time, some kind of special influence on
Liberal policy, which was certainly not the case. Although I
had fairly frequent discussions with Jo on a range of policy
questions, these were more in the field of fiscal and industrial policy and latterly about the problem of controlling
public spending, as the above excerpt suggests. Rather was
the purpose to highlight the kind of problems that had to be
resolved between education experts such as Peterson and
those economists who were beginning to penetrate the
debate about the place of 'investment in human beings' as
one of the key factors in economic development. One could
offer other and possibly better examples of the difficulties of
seeking common ground, but there is a peculiar irony about
Jo's presentation of the problem of appraising public expenditure on education. The two 'representatives' of the differing points of view were to be central figures in the
controversy that led to my withdrawal from the fringe of
Liberal politics.

Here I must pay a particular tribute to my friend, Jack
Wiseman, who joined me in York in 1964 as the Director of
the Social and Economic Research Institute. We had first of
all collaborated in writing about the economics of education
just before I left LSE where he and I had been close

colleagues from 1950 onwards.[1] Curiously enough, this was the result of an invitation to write one of the principal articles for the 1956 number of the *Yearbook of Education* on 'The Finance of State Education in the United Kingdom', that is just before *The Unservile State* essays appeared.

Our analysis of education adopted the economists' method of identifying a 'market' for a good or service, and explaining what were the forces of supply and demand at work, and the illustration of its operation by suitable data with a view to discussing the underlying trends and associated changes in the amount and structure of educational finance. The placing of education firmly under the economists' microscope was something of a shock for the editors. Still, they accepted that it was useful to be aware of alternative approaches to the study of the use of educational resources, although not entirely assured that we were not trying to persuade their clientele that we were adherents of some 'pig philosophy' which all serious scholars should oppose. (Guilt by association with any form of statistical presentation is still widespread and is reinforced by any mention of 'cost-benefit analysis'. This is particularly prevalent in appraisal of educational provision, as Jo Grimond seemed to realise!)

This incursion into economic analysis of education was the by-product of a more ambitious project that led to the appearance of what became our best known joint work, *The Growth of Public Expenditure in the United Kingdom*, first published as one of a series of studies on public sector growth and economic change by The National Bureau of Economic

---

[1]    Jack Wiseman (1920–91) in his time was one of the most colourful figures in academic economics teaching and research, missed greatly when he died so shortly after his retirement as Emeritus Professor of Economics at York. Probably the best introduction to his mind, manner and character is his own introductory essay to his collected papers. (See Chapter 1, 'Talks too much', in *Cost, Choice, and Political Economy*, Edward Elgar, 1988, pp. 1–35) He was never a member of the Liberal Party but was an early member of The Unservile State Group.

Research (NBER), New York, in 1961.[2] It was to play a crucial role in the changes that took place after my 'downfall'. I
had established overseas contacts in public finance and
public policy through my interests in European literature
that had grown out of some knowledge of French, German
and later Italian, but this joint volume with Jack gave us
both some international standing in our specialism that
later became an important element in our professional lives.
It also placed us in a position to take a more direct part in the
national debate on public finance questions and in my own
case, I suppose, to later secondment to the Department of
Trade and Industry as its Chief Economic Adviser (1973–76)
towards the end of my York appointment. In short, other
opportunities were to come my way in being 'anxious to do
good', whatever residual doubts arising from experience
with the Liberals had modified my capacity and enthusiasm to be able to do so.

## II: Market Failure and Education

We came to the study of educational policy by different
routes.[3] Our close collaboration began with a detailed criti-

---

[2]    Jack Wiseman (loc cit) offers an amusing and instructive account of
       our collaboration by the process of creative tension that led to the
       completion of this work after a gestation period of 5 years. He also
       offers a frank appraisal of what he considers is its place in the
       development of public expenditure analysis and public finance in
       general with which I fully agree. I would only add that the editorial
       process took nearly 3 years in order to meet the exacting standards of
       exposition of the NBER. We fought (and lost) the battle to preserve
       traditional English spelling!

[3]    My earlier work on national income and social accounting got me
       involved in trying to display the place of educational finance in
       public budgets. I was a member of two advisory teams, one in Ireland
       for OECD on the finance of technical education and the other in
       Afghanistan (1962) to help the government negotiate a loan from the
       Bank of Reconstruction and Development (now the World Bank)
       advised by a UNESCO appointed team. My having to make rough
       calculations of the National Income of the latter country in a period of
       two weeks is not something I readily reveal! Jack's interest arose
       from agreeing to offer a paper to the British Association on the
       economist's view of educational principles and policy, delivered in
       1958. It is the first professional discussion of educational vouchers in
       the UK. It forms an important part of our joint proposals that I had

cism of the political philosophy underpinning a famous paper by Paul Samuelson on the technical defects of the market as a mechanism in providing defence and law and order. This was because these services could not be provided in a divisible form. Once provided, those who benefited but refused to pay could not be denied the service. Why therefore should anyone pay? But non-payment would seem to prevent any provision of the service at all if individuals were free to choose — known in economics by the technical jargon as "the non-revelation of preferences problem"!

We recognized the importance and the elegance of Samuelson's exposition of the 'market failure' case and which has spawned a vast and still growing literature on the solutions to the problems to which it gives rise, and the extent to which it required government intervention. We considered that Samuelson had too readily accepted that any solution precluded the right of those who merited a direct part in the decisions taken on the amount and form of indivisible goods if only because they had to pay for them. This should presumably be left to the modern equivalent of Plato's Guardians (economists?) advising government, though some political means might be found to have the policy implications reviewed by a democratic process, eg Parliamentary approval of the taxes necessary to pay for the services.[4] Jack and I denied that the 'non-revelation of preferences problem' justified two common conclusions derived from Samuelson, viz. that the solution to the 'non-revelation of preferences problem' meant that a dictated solution was both desirable and feasible. (We wrote a criticism of Samuelson which we sent to the *Review of Economics and Statistics*, but it was rejected.)

---

later to defend from the attacks of Liberal educationists. See Jack Wiseman (1959).

[4] This summary inevitably does less than justice to the subtlety of Samuelson's argument and of the development of defences of its policy implications by a host of earnest disciples. The original Samuelson articles appeared in *The Review of Economics and Statistics*, 1954, 1955 and 1958.

We saw a chance to illustrate our criticisms in public discussion rather than in the closed circle of academic discourse, and this came in our presentation of evidence to the Robbins Committee on Higher Education (Command Paper 2154, 1963). This famous Committee, chaired by our mutual friend and mentor at LSE, Lionel Robbins, is generally credited with leading the government of the day to the rapid expansion of university education, York itself being a prime example.[5]

Before showing how our approach to the policy implications of so-called 'market failure' was based on different conclusions than the many others who saw the state playing a major role in the defining and implementation of educational policy, there is a further element in that approach that is likely to have alienated Professors of Education. The relevance of our evidence to the Robbins Committee lies in our exposition of the general purpose of education, quite apart from our specific proposals for the organisation and financing of higher education. (My retreat from close connections with the Liberal Party was signalled by the views of Jack and myself on pre-University education.) This should become clear in the introduction to our evidence, as in the reproduction of paras 1–8 in Annex 11.1 of this chapter.

Briefly, what seems to have stuck in the craw of educationists is the 'terrible' idea that there is any parallel between the educational process and the production process generally. There are teachers of economics who impart their knowledge as if it concerned higher truths only properly perceived by the penetration of mathematics of a standard that even some natural scientists are unlikely to attain. If they grade the subsequent careers of their students the highest marks are given to those who are replicas of themselves. I admit casual empiricism to be the origin of my belief that educationists of the period (circa 1960s) were

---

[5]    Lionel Robbins was also the Chairman of the Academic Planning Board for York that had been set up by the Privy Council to prepared York's Charter for government approval. As the first academic professorial appointee from a Chair elsewhere I became closely involved in the appraisal of the draft Charter.

governed by similar preconceptions of their role as educators, but were more skilful at public relations than economists. They had the advantage that somehow the disassociation of education from the sordid 'ordinary business of life' gave them a further advantage allowing them to claim some sort of moral superiority over us, and certainly greater *cachet* in public discussion of educational aims.

Perhaps these very differences in perception encouraged Jack and I to trail our coat somewhat. Consider the aforementioned passage reproduced in Annex 11.1. It can be defended on three counts against a charge of representing a 'pig philosophy':

i.    Education is viewed as an industry in which the consumer is submitted to an investment process that results in an output of benefits and, as such, has an opportunity cost. But we do recognize that the 'product' can be designed not only to improve productivity but also to foster moral and intellectual qualities of importance in preserving a democratic society.

ii.   The benefits of education, whatever the weighting as between its different 'outputs', do not accrue only to those undergoing instruction. These benefits cannot always be realised to the extent that the community desires, in which case at least a *prima facie* case can be made for some form of state intervention. As already argued, this leaves open the form of intervention and the requirement that it should not be incompatible with other components of a liberal philosophy.

iii.  The very fact that benefits other than the improvement in the productivity of the consumer are recognized as important has an important bearing on how the consumer is instructed. As a significant part of the output of education is represented by those who offer this instruction, it is willingly accepted that teaching must emphasise trust and moral integrity in its code of practice. This applies equally to economics teaching and research as to any other discipline.

However, this apologia that we took every opportunity to promulgate was far from sufficient to remove scepticism about the practice of economists. Any invasion by them of the territorial claims of prominent educationists in regard to both the principles, practice and organisation of a national system of education was to be strongly resisted.

### III: Jack and the Lobster

Concurrently with our co-operation, made even firmer by his joining me in York as Professor of Applied Economics and Director of the Social and Economic Research Institute, Jack and I had become members of the Advisory Council of the Institute of Economic Affairs (IEA). In the early 1960s that immediately earned us the label of being 'radical reactionaries', like many other primarily Marxian slogans more a term of abuse than a useful shorthand description of one's political views. Invited by its Editorial Director, Arthur Seldon (cf. Chapter 7) to develop our ideas on the finance of education, we produced *Education for Democrats*, which appeared as one of the IEA's Hobart Papers No. 25.

The publication is, as it was meant to be, a liberal economist's view of the finance of education and embodies a value judgment that is widely accepted in principle but which under close examination, leads to uncomfortable conclusions even to those who support it. That principle is that education is a service provided for those who are to be educated and that they, alone or with specific advice, are the principal judges of its value. This is the principle of consumer sovereignty.

Before putting pen to paper, we had to think our way through how to apply the principle to the actual system of British education. Although the pamphlet covers the whole range of education, it was the application to school education that was our main concern. We agreed that the principle as stated had to include some initial assumption about the question of access to education that would depend on the means available to the educated and any barriers to their choice of where and what to study.

The reader will have sensed my unease about the solution to the problem of inequality of distribution of income and capital. Jack was rather amused at this and offered his own solution. Sometime before our arrival at York we had been invited to give the lead paper at the annual conference held by the International Institute of Public Finance (IIPF), the organisation of which entailed a visit to Paris to join the Programme Committee. By some influential means the IIPF President induced our French colleagues to lay on a lunch hosted by a very up-and-coming French political economist, Giscard d'Estaing. These were the days when it was sometimes difficult to pick one's way past the prone figures wrapped up against the cold who had sought nightly shelter in the entrances to Paris's Metro Stations. When the first course appeared, we were served by waiters dressed as pre-revolutionary flunkies and who placed before us a lobster apiece. My middle class conscience troubled me greatly, thinking of the *oubliées* without a home to go to, and I turned to Jack to express my worries concerning the disparity between our opportunities and theirs. Jack—the scion of a very poor Lancastrian family, who had had to leave school at 14, attend night classes to obtain university entrance and study at home under very difficult conditions, not to speak of 5 years in the Army before reaching LSE to read for the BSc (Econ) at the age of 26—chortled. 'That is the difference between us, Alan. You would want us to be deprived of our lobster. I want *everyone* to be able to have a lobster!' He then attacked his lobster with gusto.

Of course, his riposte might be construed as a rationalisation designed to salve our consciences, but it was nothing of the sort. He genuinely believed what he said. He had offered a salutary reminder relevant to the next stage of our social policy proposals: first, that correcting inequalities of wealth, in liberal political philosophy, entailed levelling up and not levelling down; and, second, that one had a responsibility not only to define the aims of policy but to describe the *process*, and thereby the timing, of change that would be required to fulfil them and the extent to which the aims affected the educational process.

## IV: The Voucher Scheme in Context

*Education for Democrats* is a discourse on the finance of every stage of education from nursery school to university. In contrast, the determined opposition to our proposals by Liberal educationists was concentrated on our views on the finance of pre-university education.[6] Hence our concentration on financial incentives to improve access to education particularly in the case of poor families.

So, like the Classical economists, notably Adam Smith, we began with a clear belief in increasing the opportunities available for education. However, a liberal disposition, as in Smith's case, placed distinct limitations on the extent and the form of public intervention. It is worth repeating that the prime purpose of improving opportunities was to encourage individuals to a better understanding and judgment of how to improve their own welfare and that of others affected by their actions—a tall order, with finance only playing what appeared to be a humble role.

While I am sure that Jack would have felt entirely committed to this view of education, I have to offer my own perception of the finance of education within the context of a liberal social policy though recognizing that it had to take account of economic realities. This meant considering the question why should finance of education be completely separated off from a social policy with income support as its foundation rather than based on financing support to the various ways in which goods purchased out of income could be subsidised. The general case for income support has already been considered in Chapters 4 and 5, and the general approval of the case by Liberal leaders. Pursuing this matter shows that financing education in this way

---

[6]  The intrepid reader of this work will find a development of the views expressed in sections I–III of this chapter in parts III to V of our pamphlet. Our adoption of the voucher system of educational finance was influenced by a now famous proposal of Milton Friedman, 'The Role of Government in Education' in *Education and the Public Interest*, ed. Robert Solo, 1955, Rutgers University Press, and reprinted in the author's *Capitalism and Freedom*, 1962, Chicago University Press.

raised some fundamental issues that Liberals had not so far faced up to.

Consider the scheme that Jack and I developed in *Education for Democrats* for primary and secondary education. In very general terms, extending and improving them meant adjusting the existing system so that as many pupils as possible should be offered the chance to reach the standard of entry required by higher education. It was too much to suppose, given both the existing inequalities of income and wealth and the general standard of living, that this was possible by encouraging poorer parents to spend a great proportion of their income on educational services. They would also be faced with the prospect that the very children who could currently earn a substantial part of their own living would be encouraged to delay their entry into the labour market so as to continue their education to university level.

Funding the investment in education by borrowing was a remote alternative, banks and building societies being understandably unwilling to finance investment if unable to 'foreclose the mortgage' in the event of non-payment. Scholarships offered by both public institutions and private foundations were very limited in number.[7]

Our solution was a voucher worth a given sum of money to be used specifically to finance fees payable to the school or other institutions providing the service. This could be used in making payment, depending on choice of parents, to a public or private institution. In short, it was a 'tied payment', unlike general income support, but otherwise ful-

---

[7] My father, eldest son in a family of six with modest means, benefited from the so-called Lancaster scheme in operation over 100 years ago. His university fees, including laboratory fees, were paid for, the prime condition of the award being a contract that required him to become a school teacher. Actually, he was released from this obligation in becoming a University Demonstrator and, eventually, after service in the First World War in the Northumberland Fusiliers, a Lecturer in Zoology at Armstrong College, Newcastle, part of Durham University. Eventually he became Professor of Zoology, University of St Andrews, at Queen's College, Dundee (1926–56) and a Fellow of the Royal Society of Edinburgh. I have come across several of these 'indenture' systems in other parts of the world, notably in financing medical and engineering studies.

filled the general precept of encouraging freedom of choice, and could be closely related to 'ability to pay'.

It soon became clear that the voucher system is more than a very minor addition to social policy but implies a major change in the entire relationship between the state and the individual. While totally in keeping with a liberalist approach, it would entail very big changes in the perspective of Liberalism as then conceived by politicians and influential advisers. It would offer a measure of how much influence liberals really had in policy matters, albeit more in the long than in the short run.

Consider first of all the demand for education. Education provision would be largely determined by parental choices. This immediately raised the matter of parents' ability and willingness to choose the education that seemed suitable for their charges. Nothing in the voucher proposal would oppose two important pre-conditions. The first would be a role for the state in assuring that acceptable standards of education would be met, implying some form of inspection and therefore public regulation of schools. The second would be how to ensure that choices were made with sufficient unbiased information about the ability of schools to reach the required standard. This entailed a judgment on the relative merits of state provision of information or state financing of private provision or simply state regulation of private providers of such information. The ultimate aim of inspection and information provision would be to promote equalizing ability to choose that otherwise would benefit largely richer persons themselves who, if better educated, were better able to assess the advice on offer.

Next, it would be very easy to claim that if vouchers were issued to all parents they would provide a differential benefit to richer parents, who would be in a position to 'top up' vouchers. Leaving aside for the moment how such action could affect the price of education, any differential benefit of this kind could be controlled by adding the cost of the voucher to the taxable income(s) of the parents. (Family allowances, payable to parents for every child other than the first, were regarded as part of taxable income after they were introduced shortly after the end of WW2.) There can be no doubt that the distributional effects of any actual, administratively possible voucher scheme raised further questions about the existing tax arrangements affecting the demand for private education, notably the tax advantages accorded to private donations to non-profit making educational establishments.

Turning to the supply side of education, it is clear that there were marked differences between the then existing provision of education and other goods and services dependent on sales to direct customers no longer being subsidized. Close on 90% of school pupils were taught in state schools largely financed by government, notably through local authorities, so that there was no direct financial relation with the 'customers', ie children or their parents, and no control by schools over the size and structure of their budget, notably capital expenditure, and staffing conditions of pay and prospects. A change to financing of schools etc through direct payment entailed a very different organizational pattern—a point to be taken up shortly. Here one emphasises the difference with private education where there had been a long tradition of schools where school governors would be responsible for the financial arrangements, but would rely on senior employees to advise them on budgetary and administrative matters and who would supervise the execution of a school's policy.

The reader may already be speculating on what the consequences would be of matching supply and demand in such a system. The financial relationship between schools and their customers would largely depend on how the 'market' would be organized. The conditions for conforming to the principle of consumer sovereignty would not be met by simply changing the method by which schools were financed. It required that voucher users would be able to exercise a choice of school and have the right to transfer a child from one school to another because of dissatisfaction with the service provided. All well and good, of course, provided that there would be sufficient choice. Again, state intervention could be necessary to prevent monopoly action, so that no school was in a position to exploit its locational advantage or found it profitable to buy out other schools or to defeat measures designed to encourage freedom of entry for new school enterprises.

There is one striking difference between the move towards income support directed to improve educational opportunities and how such a move affected other services that had previously been subsidised. In the latter, the mode of 'production' was not affected by the change, though it might be tied to other major institutional changes. An interesting example is provided by the removal of housing subsidies and rent restriction, that later led to privatising a large part of the local authority housing stock. Occupants of property could become its owners, but their domestic arrangements could remain largely unaffected. In the former case, educational services would be 'sold' in a controlled market, but the suppliers of these services would have to experience major changes in the content with an increase in parent power taking over from political pressure.

This account of the rationale for a voucher system and our recognition of some of the problems encountered in implementation is far from complete. It already indicates the lines of attack that might be used by opponents of the ethos of the voucher system. I was soon to discover how far our attempt to anticipate their objections would lead them to do so.

## Annex 11.1:  Extract from a Memorandum submitted by Prof AT Peacock and Mr J Wiseman on 26 July 1962 on the Economics of Higher Education

1.   The purpose of this memorandum is to draw attention to certain problems that must arise in any attempt to decide what constitutes an optimum use of community resources for purposes of higher education, and by what means such optimum resource-use might best be attained.

2.   The authors are both academic economists with a special interest in public finance. This memorandum is based not only on their theoretical studies of the public finance of education[8] but also upon some practical experience of the economic appraisal of education systems in other countries, carried out for two international organisations. They would also emphasise at the outset that as the assessment of the place of higher education in the economy must inevitably rest on value judgments (as is indicated in paras. 11 and 12 below), they would describe themselves as liberals. This means that they begin from the proposition that, within limits defined below, the economic system should be designed to encourage freedom of choice by consumers. They believe that individual consumers, when confronted with the relevant issues, are good judges of their own welfare in the broadest sense and will be concerned with that of future generations. It follows that they are sceptical of a view of higher education which takes it as axiomatic that consumers are not fit to choose for themselves. On the other hand, they would repudiate any suggestion that such a view entails a 'laisser-faire' approach to problems of higher education. It will be clear from later discussion that they support a considerable measure of State participation in the finance of higher education, although they are critical of its present form.

---

[8]   See, for example, AT Peacock and J. Wiseman, 'The Finance of State Education in the UK', *International Yearbook of Education*, 1956; and J Wiseman, 'The Economics of Education', *Scottish Journal of Political Economy*, February, 1959.

*Characteristics of Provision of Higher Education*

3.    Higher education is an 'industry' like any other, but with certain particular characteristics. There is no tangible product, but the industry makes an important contribution to the transmission and the improvement of human knowledge and in a form which has obvious economic significance.[9] The 'product' of higher education is designed both to improve the skill of the professional labour force directly and to foster intellectual and moral qualities which are necessary to preserve a democratic society, and which may also bring economic benefit by its influence upon the productivity of others.

4.    As an 'industry' it has certain unusual characteristics. Firstly, the 'consumer', the student, supplies his own raw material — himself — so that he foregoes earning a living (except perhaps in vacations) in order to invest in his person.

5.    Secondly, higher education is both a producer and a consumer good. It is a producer good in the sense that it is a necessary 'input' for the production of a whole range of goods and services comprising the national product, and thus an important cost of production. Unlike other production costs, the costs of the 'input' of higher education are only to a limited extent directly borne by industry. As an 'input' it is like machinery in that the skills acquired through higher education can be applied over a considerable period of time, although they may also be subject, like all investment, to depreciation and obsolescence. It is a consumer good in the sense that part of the 'output' of higher education does not contribute to the production of to-day's or to-morrow's output but is currently being enjoyed like other goods by consumers. The distinction in practice cannot be clear-cut. Thus as we shall argue in detail below, it is very difficult to determine the exact relationship between changes in the amount

---

[9]    Recent econometric studies of the forces determining the rate of economic growth in industrial countries have supported this view. See, for example, Odd Aukrust, 'Investment and Economic Growth', *Productivity Measurement Review*, No. 16, February, 1959.

and composition of national output and changes in the volume of resources used in the provision of higher education. Furthermore, insofar as people seek higher education for the non-economic benefits it confers, it is highly doubtful whether these benefits are 'used up' in the period during which they have been provided.

6.    Thirdly, its benefits, economic or non-economic, do not accrue solely to those who undergo the process of instruction. This means that they cannot always be realised to the extent that the community desires through the ordinary process of the market. All other possible reasons apart, this must necessitate some kind of participation by the State in the provision of higher education. In fact, in most advanced countries universities and other institutions of higher education are subsidised by the State or local governments, as well as by voluntary means, and the consumers of education are frequently subsidised by grants, bursaries and loans at low rates of interest. The Committee will obviously be familiar with the extent to which subsidisation on both the production and consumption side of the account has proceeded in the UK; this is reflected in the pronounced decline in fees as a source of university revenue over the last thirty years and in the large increase in the proportion of students over the same period who have been enabled to finance the major part of their studies from grants. However, acceptance of State participation in the provision of higher education does not imply that all forms of participation are equally acceptable; particularly, the fact that the State has an interest in the matter does not displace the direct interest of individuals in their own education. In the case of Britain, we shall argue below that while we are in favour of State participation on a considerable scale, we are dissatisfied with the form that participation currently takes, and believe that other methods of intervention would be superior.

7.    Fourthly and finally, a significant part of the 'output' of higher education is absorbed by the educational sector itself, so that any expansion of higher education for the purposes of improving our economic performance has a 'feed-back' effect which is manifested in an increased

demand for university teachers and researchers. This fact is of some importance in any attempt to draw up a manpower budget which is consistent with the economic objectives sought by the community.

8.    We are aware that our description of higher education as an industry stresses the obvious, but perhaps we can be forgiven for describing its characteristics in detail because they provide an essential framework for our discussion and have a bearing on the form and content of our recommendations.

# Chapter 12

# The End is Nigh

### I: The (In)Significance of Change

It may seem odd to the reader that this book begins with the presentation of the author's aspirations in terms of a wide spectrum of policy issues that became part of the drama of post-WW2 politics, but finishes not with a bang but with something less than a whimper. To abandon a political cause over such an apparently trivial matter as the non-acceptance of what appears to be a modest proposal regarding educational finance does not seem either a sensible reason for deserting it or a matter of any consequence to those engaged in the cut and thrust of public debate. More-over, not much public attention was likely to be paid to the disagreements of an obscure Professor from outside the golden triangle of British academia with the executives of the remains of what was once a potent political force.

I was bound to consider this assessment, but I sensed at the time of leaving the Liberals in any advisory capacity that there was much more to it than simply a minor spat — not even perhaps more than a friendly disagreement — in which it might be claimed that I had acted in a rather impetuous and, some might say childish, manner.

Jack Wiseman and I had emphasised the changes that a successful system for widening educational choice would require as being mainly associated with a concurrent improvement in its quality. We had concentrated on the growing influence to be exerted by demand on the *process* of change. While this in itself would have a major effect on the system of educational finance, it was not balanced by close

consideration of the necessary institutional changes that
would have to take place in the organisation of educational
services. Vouchers would not only increase the power of
'consumers'. They would introduce competition between
schools. We made it clear that this would make schools
better aware that their standards were under scrutiny,
although this would depend on the absence of 'natural
monopoly' when guarantees of freedom of entry in provision of alternative sources of education would be ineffec-
tive.

The emphasis on creating a 'market' for school education
as a necessary element in the working of a voucher system
must postulate that major adjustments would be necessary
in the supply of educational services. Schools and colleges
would have to be responsive to parental preferences which
in turn would depend on the price and perceived quality of
the services on offer. Assessment of the quality of teaching,
for example, would no longer depend solely on the guarantees offered by government under pressure from voters on
local or national politicians called upon to vote on educational budgets. They would need to be directly conveyed to
parents and guardians able to 'vote with their feet' and
gaining practice in assessing the value of sources of information. In short, far reaching managerial changes were postulated that presaged a kind of cultural revolution.

It was also clear from the stir created by the voucher idea
that it might be further extended to other government-pro-
vided services such as health services and cultural services
provided by museums and galleries and, at the local level,
to housing.[1] One might further extend speculation to consider a related and more radical change derived from the

[1]    Note the important difference between such schemes, as applied to
       services that it was not compulsory to buy, and education. An
       educational voucher is easily made non-transferable. As soon as a
       voucher system is applied to voluntary purchases there is the
       prospect of a 'market' in vouchers in which non-users can sell them.
       The benefit of the scheme is then less likely to accrue to those for
       whom it is designed. I investigated this difference and the possible
       ways of overcoming transferability much later in trying to develop a
       practicable scheme for encouraging consumer support for the

older liberal tradition of the Classical economists by considering, in a modern context, what were the proper functions of the state and the extent fulfilling these really made the existing methods of provision, with its emphasis on nationalization of production, as inviolable.[2] In the narrative and commentary that follows, it would seem as if the differences between the liberal economists' approach to the finance of welfare services that considered that far reaching changes should be instituted in the functions of government and the educationists and their supporters, including politicians, lay primarily in the practicability of our recommendations. I am arguing that there was something more, something fundamental, in the differences. Those who rejected the Peacock-Wiseman proposals were probably more aware than I was that more was at stake than the introduction of a marginal change in the Liberal party programme for reform of the welfare estate.[3]

## II: The Process of Rejection

The publication of *Education for Democrats* caused a certain amount of turbulence in the academic world and, in the growing politicisation of academic life, Jack and I were labelled as extreme right-wingers, albeit of a radical disposition. Serious professional discussion had to wait until the 1970s when the distributional implications of the Samuelsonian approach to public economics (cf above, Chapter 9) became the source of speculation amongst economists who

---

performed arts—see *Paying The Piper*, Edinburgh University Press, Chapter 7.

[2]    I had floated the idea of privatizing local government housing in *The Welfare Society* (1961), and this pre-dates its extensive introduction in the early 1980s. I hedged it round with the proviso that the sale of houses should be on very long leases, so giving local authorities a residual control over land use by remaining the ground landlords. This would be regarded as being over-cautious today!

[3]    The up-and-coming Liberal John Pardoe was shortly after this period to write a defence of Selective Welfare Provision which paid particular attention to the need for radical changes in the organisation of production of services made necessary to conform to the acceptance of consumer choice. See the Liberal Party monthly publication *New Outlook*, No. 69, September 1967.

disputed its policy relevance. This side of the welfare debate would take us too far away from my central theme, which was unaffected by the esoteric gymnastics of economic theorists.[4]

The debates on education in the Liberal Party, being tied very much to the immediate necessity of attracting voters to their cause, required some means of differentiating its product from that of other parties. So far as vouchers were concerned, they were treated with hostility by Labour educationists whose prime interest in economic questions was to lobby for a massive increase in public expenditure on both teaching and research. Conservatives relied on their traditional hostility to academic 'speculation' and the usual associated *ad hominem* arguments designed to question the right of academics to claim any knowledge of the real world.

At least it may be said that the Liberal Party Executive encouraged a much more serious and extended debate on the financial issues, a tribute perhaps to the efforts of the Unservile State Group and their respect for Elliot Dodds, its Chairman, and the politician members of the Group, notably Jo Grimond, then still leader of the Parliamentary party, and latterly Richard Wainwright.

The public debate began in rather an odd fashion through Peterson's review (January 1966 number of *New Outlook*) of Eddie West's remarkable book *Education and the State*, which appeared shortly after *Education for Democrats*. In his review Peterson pinpointed vouchers as a dangerous threat to Liberal educational policy. He did not appear to have heard of our work, or ignored it, and no doubt this influenced the aggrieved tone of my criticism of his position

---

[4]    Curiously enough, overseas interest did not confirm that we had adopted some distinct political position. It came to our notice that our Paper has been commended in a pastoral letter of the Bishop of Lisbon on the one hand, and by the Vice Minister of Education for the Socialist State of Bulgaria on the other. The Vice Minister paid us a special visit to York and averred that he believed in the principle that pupils and students should pay for their education. I have not traced his subsequent career.

which was published in *New Outlook* in April 1966 — Exhibit 1 in the ensuing debate (see Annex 12).

My arguments were a repetition of parts of *Education for Democrats* but with a different emphasis in order to counter Peterson's assertions. (I need not repeat these, and Exhibit 1 can be read very rapidly.) What I did not realise was that an attack on Peterson raised fundamental issues about Liberal approaches to educational provision that had not so far been questioned. Richard Lamb in a later number of *New Outlook* maintained that Peacock/Wiseman arguments divided the Executive. Some members wanted them to be rejected and to be given no space in Liberal publications to their promulgation. Others, including even those who opposed the arguments themselves, took the position that suppression would be an illiberal move. What prevailed in this debate was the continuation of discussion in subsequent numbers of *New Outlook*. Peterson offered a courteous reply suggesting that the case against his position was at least well argued (see Exhibit 2 in Annex 12). Michael Fogarty and John Pardoe defended us, the latter even envisaging the extension of vouchers to a whole range of social policies and also to the reorganization of the supply of social services to simulate competitive conditions in their provision. I was unaware at the time that Arthur Seldon, remembered by older Liberals as an associate of the much-respected Elliot Dodds, was to address the Liberal Assembly of 1966 in Brighton. He expounded the case for vouchers with vigour and vivacity, but, curiously, made no comment on the Peacock/Wiseman proposals.

However, I could have no expectations that our proposals would be adopted as part of official policy. Defeat was inevitable when the President of the Liberal Party had already damned them (but in the nicest possible way) in the May 1966 number of *New Outlook* (reproduced as Exhibit 3, in Annex 12). It was hard to take because the President was now my old friend and colleague, Nancy Seear, Lecturer in Personnel Management, LSE. She makes two very striking assertions that were something of a surprise. The first was that 'I just do not .believe that full freedom of choice is

something which in the interests of the child, can be left
largely to the parent. Nor do I see any particular reason that
as time goes on, and with practice and increasing prosperity, parents will get better.' (Clearly, she shared the views on
parentage expressed in Philip Larkin's famous poem!) The
second was that 'good schools would get bigger and better
but for many generations of school children the bad schools
would not be eliminated'.

A social scientist, at least nowadays, would seek some
means of testing such assertions and, although design
might be a problem, of devising some experiment to see
whether a voucher scheme might work, such as trying it out
in a particular area. Even if such a scheme ran into difficulties of a practical nature, one might learn something important for policy purposes. With no prospect of reaching the
stage where proof were considered desirable or feasible, the
only thing to do would be to agree to differ. I was not in a
position to argue the point and to persuade Nancy that she
might be mistaken and that, in turn, I might be persuaded, if
not to change my mind, to consider in more detail how freedom of choice could be made to accord with a desire to
improve educational quality. For both of us the opportunity
cost of continuing the argument was too high.

I made one more attempt to lay out the general approach
to a liberal policy for the provision and finance of welfare
services. About the same time as this argument about the
specific question of the finance of education, I had summa-
rised my views on the 'political economy of welfare' in an
article under that name. It was an extension of some ideas in
*The Welfare Society* and published in *The Three Banks Review*
some time before in December, 1964. My audience was to be
the Parliamentary Party and the invitation having origi-
nated from Jo Grimond and Richard Wainwright. I cannot
recall the date, but remember that we met sometime in the
early evening in the famous St Stephen's Tavern. My presentation excited little discussion and I sensed that the Party
MPs may have felt that they had heard enough about the
welfare state, current concerns of the House of Commons
being more focused on such matters as Britain's poor

growth performance and on our balance of payments problems. It became a dispiriting occasion and although everyone was friendly and courteous, they had difficulty in displaying the rapt attention to my exposition that I had hoped for.

So there was a decision to be made. I would clearly be more useful and influential, if only to a minor degree, if I concentrated more on general economic matters. After all, if I was to fulfil the role of Frank Paish before me, more help would be sought with developing policies more in line with the Liberal Party's perceptions of what would gain them more credibility with the electorate. I was not offered the opportunity to express my views on such matters as Labour's grandiose economic planning structure or on their methods for resolving balance of payments crises, although I did discuss such matters now and again with Jo. (We were to follow this procedure of occasional meetings and correspondence right up to his retirement from politics and even beyond.)

### III: Retreat

The reader can be spared some elaborate, inevitably egocentric, post-mortem. It was something of a wrench to cease to have any regular contact with the Liberals but there were other considerations than hurt pride for withdrawal.

Much was happening in the development of both economic analysis and its applications that required my attention at the head of a vigorous and lively department of economists, economic historians and statisticians. It would do neither myself nor my colleagues any good if I did not have a professional standing sufficient for them to want to stay and to accept the opportunity of disagreeing with me and my professorial confreres over research, pedagogic and promotional matters. More time had to be sought to get my economics in good repair. (I did not altogether agree with Jack Wiseman that we should be making good decisions if, once having a clear idea that our junior colleagues had the necessary intellectual abilities, an important criterion for their appointment and promotion would be our inability to understand any longer what they were talking about!)

The public and international concern for improving the prospects of the poor intensified in the 1960s and governments and international agencies looked towards economics departments for help in the assessment and execution of aid programmes. With some residual reputation of expertise in assessing the economic condition and the structure of developing countries (see Chapter 3 above) and a niche in the network of professional contacts I had come under considerable pressure to give advice on organizational and recruitment matters. Jack and I certainly agreed that good young economists and statisticians became even better ones if they went through the experience of being consultants working to a time table and having to produce results with firm deadlines — and being paid at the rates which provided a degree of supplementation of their meagre salaries sufficient for us to be able to keep them in academic life! Moreover, a new, young university was expected to provide ample evidence of a 'wish' — not 'an anxiety' — to do good! The frustrations of political advice-giving made this competing attraction in the use of professional skill inviting, though it is an open question how one assesses the result was an increase in the welfare of humankind. A map of where York economists and statisticians took part in this form of advice-giving in those times would cover 15 different countries from Peru and Puerto Rico to Malaysia and Malawi.

There is a degree of rationalisation in this change in the direction of my career. Political parties in the UK, including the Liberals, could not be unaware of a changing world where advice on economic matters depended on what time some committed member of the party could devote to do more than offer off-the-cuff perceptions of the line that might be taken in some Parliamentary debate or enquiry. A more permanent arrangement would be necessary to shadow the growth in the professionalism of economic advice within the government machine. How extensive and highly organized this had become was made clear to me some years later when I went on secondment to become Chief Economic Adviser to the Department of Trade and Industry (1973–76). The slender resources of the Liberal Party might not extend to anything resembling the Treasury's administrative capability. It could provide for some basic number-crunching, and monitoring of government publications by the odd research assistant or two.

Nothing was actually said to suggest that I had been declared redundant, but it was clear that the shift in emphasis amongst the perplexing economic problems of the day called for help from economists with an established reputation in international economics. I could not claim to fill the bill.

By co-incidence, the economist who did fill the bill had just been appointed by us as Lecturer in Economics at York—John Williamson, who took a First at LSE in International Economics and had recently completed his PhD at Princeton. I cannot speak too highly of him as an economist, colleague and friend. He was then as now a brilliant expositor and only too willing to put this great quality to the benefit of Liberalism.

We had many friendly arguments that lead a member of the Department, questioned on its collective political orientation, to describe it as 'covering the whole spectrum of contemporary political thinking with a Liberal at either end!' I am only tempted to add that we used to swap positions from time to time just to add confusion to the attempt to stereotype us, and that our disagreements centred more on the capacity of governments and more specifically the civil service to act as the dispassionate, all-seeing and unselfish guardians of the public weal that he believed we could take for granted. I was almost sorry when some years later he adopted a much more sceptical view of our civil service and of international organizations and was disposed to agree with me. The Liberals were extremely lucky to have him so willing to help them develop an international trade and payments policy and he was much better than I was in expounding his views, as he did, in public debate. It would have been foolish for me ever to have believed that I had been other than temporarily useful and that any discernible gap in available advice could not be filled. I was lucky to have had the opportunity and for such a long period to assuage my anxiety to do good even if I had failed in my mission.

## Annex 12
### Exhibit 1: Professor Alan Peacock
*Give parents vouchers and let them choose schools*

It is unfortunate that Alec Peterson's criticism of the voucher system for education should be based on recent works, important and interesting in themselves, in which it receives only incidental mention, and does not do Professor Wiseman and myself the honour of referring to our *Education for Democrats* in which the scheme was first fully worked out with particular reference to Britain. What he describes as a voucher scheme is almost unrecognisable to me and his attempt to dismiss it as anti-Liberal, while laced with some amusing comments, seems to he based on a series of misunderstandings.

Any defence of the voucher system must begin by considering the economics of a Liberal social policy. The Liberal ideal relevant to such a policy is individual self-development within a free society. This places a heavy burden on the shoulders of the family, which, as Hobhouse pointed out, must he 'of the strongest independent vitality' if Liberalism is to survive. Now a sceptical view is taken of the family as the agent for the preservation and improvement of the quality of living, particularly by sonic sociologists and educationalists – possibly also by Alec Peterson. There is good reason for this. One is obviously the lack of means but this is not the main reason for scepticism. The family is faced with a complex and rapidly changing social environment which it cannot readily influence and in which the technical knowledge required to make wise spending decisions – which consumer durable to buy (which commit one to spending out of an uncertain future income), which occupation to choose for oneself and one's children and how to change one's occupation in the face of redundancy – is becoming more difficult to grasp.

Whatever the deficiencies of the family may be, and they may be particularly important in choices about education, the cornerstone of a Liberal social policy should surely not he to divest the family of the responsibility for taking most of the important decisions which affect its well-being, but to help them to improve the decisions themselves.

A *sine qua non* of sensible individual decision-making is an adequate standard of living as measured by the size of household incomes. This is accepted Liberal policy and nothing more need be said about it. What we need to turn our attention to is the *quality* of spending out of income, and the obvious Liberal way of effecting improvements in quality is by the encouragement of all kinds of information services, including those dealing with educational facilities, which help to protect and advise the consumer.

Obviously, this is not believed to be enough. Otherwise we would not encourage nor insist upon insurance subsidised by the fiscal system for sickness, old-age and unemployment so that people redistribute their income through time in order to synchronise needs and means. The voucher falls into this kind of category of fiscal measures by recognising that education is so important to everyone that the very least we can do is to car mark funds provided to the family for the provision of education, and funds which can only be spent for that purpose. It is like a family allowance which can only be spent on one specific item of expenditure and, in a world in which the inequality of incomes and wealth are considered intolerable, it could, like the family allowance, he regarded as part of taxable income.

## Fees For All State Schools

It is first and foremost a *mechanism* and the amount of the voucher could he varied according to the community's valuation of the social benefits which different amounts and types of education are estimated to provide. (This point is entirely overlooked by Alec Peterson.) The voucher could be used for the payment of fees at any public or private school, subject to certain restrictions to be mentioned, an important corollary being that state-provided schools would be fee-paying and would not be subsidised out of the rates.

The essence of the system. then, is that there would be massive state support for education, but no presumption that the state should monopolise the provision of educational facilities. On the other hand there are some important preliminary measures which would have to be undertaken before the scheme could be operated. even in a modified form. The public authorities would have to inspect and accredit all schools for which the voucher could he used. Any form of financial discrimination which favoured private education at the outset would have to be removed. For example, given the present dissatisfaction with the distribution of income and wealth, one might abolish educational convenants which enable the rich to finance a child's fees by a reduction in their tax obligations and sub-standard state schools may be given once-and-for-all capital grants in order to improve buildings.

The important advantage of this system is that it removes financial barriers which prevent the access of all to education according to their ability and interests. Moreover, subject to the important rule of accreditation, the very diversity of education provision, public and private, would ensure that there was a real choice between alternatives which would offer an incentive to schools to provide good service. Nothing could be worse than the present situation in which the choice is often one local state school with very little real chance of transfer (and then often only after considerable trouble) to another state school. The other alternative is only open to the relatively affluent — to pay the rates to finance other children's education and to pay the full price of a private education. There is nothing between paying nothing and paying the earth. This is hardly the kind of situation which will encourage parental interest in doing the best they can for their children.

There is a more fundamental point than this. While an educational policy must exercise surveillance over private and public sector alike in order to ensure that there is at least a common denominator of tolerance and understanding being taught in them, it is important in a Liberal society not to risk the danger of ignoring minority views even in matters of education both in respect of educational techniques and philosophy. A complete state monopoly of education may too easily be dominated by conventional ideas.

Two aspects of the scheme worry Alec Peterson. One is 'glossy' advertising schools calculated to induce susceptible parents to use their vouchers in inefficient ways. This could be a difficulty if there were no accreditation of schools and no means available to control 'percussive' methods of advertising. But surely these controls could be exercised. As it is, the HMC schools agree not to advertise in the Press and it might even be possible to enforce good standards in the provision of genuine information by voluntary means. What strikes me about the present situation is the simple *lack* of information of the most crucial kind provided by state schools. I have recently tackled a few of those in authority in the provision of state schools and they have agreed with me that it may indeed be difficult for the parent to find out without considerable effort what precisely is the educational career open to an individual child from entry to a secondary school to his exit by the various doors leading to further education or to a career. I was told by one of them (and I hope that this is not a representative view) that the provision of information of this sort was 'something of a privilege' for parents. It is surely a right.

## The Rich Can Always Have More

The second doubt of Alec Peterson raises more fundamental issues. The voucher provides for minimum standards which could be generous ones and need not imply that the more intelligent pupils necessarily receive a greater 'input' of financial resources than others. This is a matter of general educational policy. There would be nothing to prevent parents, if they wished, supplementing the voucher out of their own means. Thus he argues that private provision coupled with public finance must discriminate in favour of the rich, since they are subsidised but would buy education for their children anyway. The earlier argument takes care of part of the problem—treat the vouchers as part of taxable income of parents and abolish covenants. Beyond this, we still have, as Alec Peterson stresses, a conflict between equality, in a particular sense, and liberty. The rich can in any case buy more of everything than the poor. We can alter this state of affairs by general policies directed at a more equal distribution of wealth. But let us assume that there is not going to be completely equal distribution of income and wealth (which not even left-wing Socialists support), should we prevent people from supplementing the vouchers? Apart from the question of principle, nothing but the most Draconian measures could bring this about, including in the extreme case, the prohibition of education conducted by parents in the home. *Uniform* as distinct from reasonable minimum standards could only be approximated by provision of educational facilities solely by the state. This is implied by Alec Peterson's argument, but is it what he wants?

I have already given reasons why diversity may he preferred to monopoly of education by the state and consider them sufficient for me to prefer liberty in the purchase of educational facilities to uniformity. As it is, wealth is not the only deciding factor in the supplementation of the voucher. Even relatively poor parents in an environment in which choice and diversity become a reality, might prefer to supplement vouchers than to raise their stakes on bingo. Finally, if we have any confidence in the performance of the British economy in the long run, we could expect the expansion in incomes to offer increasing opportunity to spend more on education, either through the voucher system financed by taxes on income, or through supplementation which the increase in general prosperity would allow.

It needs stressing, finally, that this kind of scheme could have many variants. It need not prevent other forms of subsidisation to state-run or private schools by the state. It might be applied to secondary education and not to primary education. And after all, it is not a crack-pot scheme hatched in an ivory tower by unwordly professors. A modified version of it is in operation in Holland and, nearer home, it is as well to remember that there has been no outcry in Scotland about the continuation until this day of fee-paying state schools in some areas. It is a Liberal scheme and deserves, I hope, a better run for its money than Alec Peterson would have us believe.

### Exhibit 2: Alec Peterson, Liberal Spokesman on Education, *Vouchers not Suitable for Schools*

It was certainly unfortunate that the discussion of Vouchers for Welfare which flourished with such animation in *New Outlook* earlier this year should have been sparked off by my review of Dr. West's *Education and the State*. In the first place it limited the field initially to that of education, perhaps the least promising area for the introduction of choice in welfare, and secondly it excluded consideration of important earlier writing on the topic. However the debate did broaden out and now that a good many people have had their say on a variety of topics it might be a good thing to assess the areas of agreement and the possibilities of reaching an acceptable and realistic policy within the party as a whole. Certainly the clashes between Professor Townsend and Mr Crossman over the present functioning of the Beveridge Welfare State indicate that any party which could satisfy both itself and the country that it had a new policy which would both increase the area of choice and raise the real level of welfare at the bottom end of the scale would be doing a national service.

It is the combination of these two aims that seems to me (not an economist) to be the crux of the economist's problems (I shall return to the administrators' problems later). The fundamental hesitation in Nancy Seear's position seems to me to be the doubt whether we have yet reached an acceptable basic minimum of welfare, financed out of taxation and available to all, into which the added but expensive value of greater choice could be built. There can be little doubt that freer choice is a liberal objective: there can also be little doubt that in the field of welfare it is more expensive. Or does any macro-economist contend that luncheon vouchers and the free competition of the market can provide a nourishing meal for the same number of people, schoolchildren or industrial workers, with no greater total diversion of resources than school or works canteens? I do not know. Perhaps they do.

If so we need to be presented with a more detailed case. If we were already an 'affluent' society there would probably be no differences within the Liberal Party on this issue. But are we? Arthur Seldon's reply to my suggestion that even if primary poverty had been eliminated in Surrey it certainly had not been in Glasgow, was that Glasgow parents might be given larger education vouchers than Surrey parents. It is an ingenious idea, equivalent of course to larger Exchequer grants to the needier authorities under the present system, but if the cost of the vouchers is to be met from general taxation, is that form of redistribution likely to be more acceptable politically than differentiation in teachers' salaries, and in money made available for rebuilding of schools, between the different areas?

The whole tenor of the criticisms made by Professor Townsend and Professor Abel Smith of the present levels of welfare is that we are below, and continuously falling further below, the acceptable minimum. Professors Fogarty, Peacock and Wiseman are not, of course, bound by the argument that the introduction of a greater degree of free choice necessarily increases the cost of welfare services. They may argue either that it does not, though, as I have said, this would have to be demonstrated more clearly, in the field of education at least, than it has been; or that, although more expensive, it would tap the resources of private spending to such an extent as to compensate for the extra cost. This latter is a very attractive argument. It seems quite wrong that the State should provide all the services which people really *need* for the welfare of themselves and their families, so that, being positively inhibited from contributing to these ends from their own resources, they are almost forced into spending their free money on bingo and candyfloss. The question which is so difficult to decide is what proportion of their private resources people really would devote to such good causes, and whether it would compensate for the loss of economics of scale which would surely follow from the dismantling of a common general state provision. It is usually argued, as Mr. Seldon did at Brighton, that in order to get them to do so and to do so wisely, a considerable campaign of public information would be necessary.

*Cost of Informing Parents*

This is another area where it seems to me that we shall have to do a bit more detailed thinking. How much would such a campaign cost? How effective would it be? How much would it add therefore to the cost of the welfare services provided through a free market? And what would be the position of a government conducting such a campaign if the rival welfare services, e.g. pensions schemes or schools, were competing in such a market? Professor Peacock maintains that adequate 'information' about different schools is a parents' 'right'; and this presumably means that some impartial public authority should provide it. What would be the position of a public authority which attempted to provide such information now about rival petrol companies or detergents? I don't say the problem is insoluble but if we are really to adopt the vouchers for welfare system we shall have to be ready with an answer.

Let me turn now to the administrative problems. It seems to me that free choice and voucher systems are most easy to introduce in areas where the welfare provided is highly mobile and does not involve static capital plant, e.g. in the payment of pensions. They are most difficult where they involve heavy and static capital equipment, e.g. in the provision of schools. It is true that people are now able and ready to travel greater distances than they were in order to take advantage of a particular welfare service, but there is a limit to this. There are many country districts where it would be grossly uneconomic and therefore unattractive to entrepreneurs to provide more than even one school at which the vouchers could be used, without involving the children in an amount of travelling which would be both bad for them and costly to their parents. There are many more where the choice would be restricted to two or three.

Moreover schools change very quickly with changes of head teacher or staff and the cost of continually expanding or contracting provision in order to make realistic the elements of parental choice might well exceed the additional resources brought in by tapping private spending. If in what I might call a three school radius School A proved very successful and so expanded to such an extent that Schools B and C went bankrupt, and if then School A declined in vigour under a less able or an ageing head, the last state of those parents would be worse than the first. This model assumes of course that the provision of schools as well as their operation is ultimately returned to the free market.

## How Much Advertising?

The great unresolved question about the voucher schemes in so far as they affect education is whether their supporters expect them to meet provision or only operation. If it is expected that, provided enough purchasing power were pumped into education through vouchers, individual entrepreneurs would assume the function of providing schools, then I still find it very hard to believe that the economies of scale would not lead to control by as small a number of entrepreneurs as now control filling stations, supermarkets or newspapers. It is all very well for Mr. Seldon to say this is a 'self-induced nightmare' but he does not say why the economic forces which operate elsewhere should not operate in the provision of schools. Would this kind of monopoly really give the parent any more free choice than the present monopoly of the local education authority, tempered by the independent school? And under what terms would these educational chains compete? Would they be forbidden to advertise as Mr. Seldon suggested in *New Outlook* or encouraged to do so as was suggested in 'Choice in Welfare'? If they advertise how much will it add to the cost of education? What guarantee have we that, as with private bus companies, any entrepreneur will bother to serve the less economically attractive areas or will not go bankrupt if he does? All these are questions which ought surely to be answered by anyone who advocates the complete return of education to the free market. After all it is a very large industry and Professor Galbraith in his Reith lectures is in the process of reminding us how very imperfect is the market in very large industries and how inevitable it is that they should be 'planned'.

## Popular Schools Raise Fees

Or do we consider that some sort of public authority should still be responsible for the planning, for ensuring that school buildings are provided in the right places to meet the needs of the future population, but that their management should be turned over to private enterprise financed through vouchers? This would at least preserve the public authority as the provider of services, inspectors, advisors and in-service training, which only the largest chains would be able to finance under the other system, but it poses problems of its own. If Authority A builds an eight form entry school in neighbourhood B, and then finds that the independent operator to whom it has given the concession is so inefficient that the numbers drop to four form entry, while parents attracted either by better education or by better advertising (or 'information' or 'prestige') are crowding out a school built for a four form entry five miles away, what will it do? If it expands the popular school to meet demand, the empty class rooms in the unpopular school will then become an unproductive cost to the education authority and so will the empty class rooms in the popular school when, as so often happens, the winds of favour change. If it does not the popular school will presumably either raise fees or 'entrance requirements'. The first would gradually lead to the split between education for the poor and education for the rich which Mr. Seldon thinks is another figment of my imagination, and the second would reintroduce the 11+.

I would like to see a system of greater choice in education introduced from the university end, as Professors Peacock and Wiseman argue in 'Education for Democrats', based on more realistic fees, less subsidies to institutions and more to individuals, and the substitution of open loans for maintenance repayable at a later stage through PAYE, rather than mean-tested grants; but the more I look at vouchers as a means of financing a school system which has to be universal, compulsory and heavily capitalised the greater the administrative difficulties and the risks of private monopolies appear. I am ready, indeed eager, to be convinced, but I doubt if either I or any other member of the party concerned with the actual administration of education will be until clear answers have been worked out to some of the practical questions I have raised.

### Exhibit 3:  Nancy Seear, President Liberal Party, *How Much Opting Out of State Welfare?*

In January *New Outlook* Alec Peterson (Liberal spokesman on education) condemned welfare vouchers. In April *New Outlook* Professor Fogarty (Liberal spokesman on social security) and Professor Peacock took Alec Peterson's arguments to pieces.

Before we get bogged down in a first-class vouchers row, let us take a long, cool look at the proposals put forward by Professors Fogarty and Peacock, who are not, in fact, a couple of ignorant reactionaries. This is especially necessary for Liberals such as me, who instinctively reject their conclusions. It could be that the likes of me are emotionally committed to a relatively static view of the Welfare State which will look quaintly but expensively irrelevant by the year 2000.

Let us make no mistake about it, in a great deal of the Professors' articles there is much that is true and also Liberal — Liberal and also true. Liberals do want wider choice: we do fear the concentration of power and control: we do want to encourage individual responsibility. It is certainly true that the country needs to spend more money on both education and the health services. It is also almost certainly true that with growing prosperity parents would be willing to spend some of their additional income on education if they did not have to choose between paying nothing at all or paying the bankrupting sums that the fully independent sector must perforce demand. There is also something more than a little absurd in the sight of parents dishing out large sums for their children to go on foreign tours, worthy though this exercise may be, when the same children attend schools with vastly overcrowded classes, inadequate libraries and appalling buildings. Parents might well choose to alter the priorities if they had any say in the matter.

It is important too, that Liberal eyes should penetrate the fog, some of it deliberate smoke screen, which characterises the present political climate. We are undeniably a class-conscious country. Class divisions are often strongly felt and there is no doubt that we need to narrow these class differences. But no society has ever existed which has not had some form of class structure and modification of class feeling should not be regarded as the over-riding purpose of every aspect of social policy. Moreover, it seems likely that Labour politicians, having lost their faith in public ownership, are gratefully fostering the problem of class as an emotionally satisfactory substitute. It is also important not to be caught by the ridiculous argument that no-one ought to have anything unless it is equally available to everyone. This line of reasoning leads to the conclusion that the only things a man should be allowed to buy are the things that no-one really wants very much. The argument itself is pretty sinister, since it can only be seriously advanced by people who never allow their eyes to rove outside these islands. To apply it to the world at large would undoubtedly solve the problem of how to improve the welfare state. On that sort of 'fair shares for all' basis there would be no additions of any kind, at least until the world population explosion had blown itself out.

On grounds such as these I am entirely in favour of applying the Professors' arguments in the field of pensions. I believe the Liberal Party has been right to come out in favour of a high basic pension for all and to have no truck with graduated schemes and compulsory state superannuation. Liberals are determined to see that no old people live in poverty. Of course there is the school of thought which says that poverty is an entirely relative term — that as has been alleged 'in a world in which some people have a Jaguar it is poverty to have an Austin Seven'. I think this is irresponsible nonsense, and I think we should say so, difficult though precise definitions of poverty undoubtedly are. It is the State's job to see old people do not live in poverty, and, as Liberals have demanded, to see that this basic minimum pension rises with rising national prosperity. But it is one of the few certain facts in life that we shall all either die or live to pension age and it is up to people who can afford it to make additional provision for themselves, encouraged, if you like, but certainly not compelled by a paternalistic state.

While I go with the Professors along what I take to be their path for the aged, after this I begin to part company, particularly in the field of education.

Alan Peacock's article, as one would expect, is closely and cogently argued. On his assumptions it cannot be faulted, but he over-simplifies the problem, and the issues he leaves out are in fact the crux of the educational dilemma.

## No Opting Out from State Education

It is, of course, true that it is purely a matter of mechanics not of principle whether the State provides education free, or whether it gives parents vouchers to enable them to buy educational services. But the education a child gets depends on two things: on the wisdom with which parents choose, and on the availability of enough really good education to go round. Now I fear I do not share Alan Peacock's confidence in parental choice. The family is, I agree, an immensely important institution, but it has often been and still is in some ways not infrequently both ignorant and a tyranny. In education, the individual concerned, the child, is not exercising choice. It is the parent who exercises it for him, and it is still true that the most important choice anyone makes is the choice of his parents. I just do not believe that full freedom of educational choice is something which in the interests of the child, can be left largely to the parent.

Nor do I see any particular reason to believe that as time goes on, and with practice and increasing prosperity, parents will get better. Each new generation of parents has to start from scratch. Some of the most astoundingly awful choices are made by some of the most affluent parents. Just look at what generations of well-to-do parents have done to their daughters. I know of at least one family who at this moment is painfully squeezing out £600 a year to disqualify their daughter for all known employment except the over-crowded occupation of money spender to a fantastically wealthy husband. In short, I just do not believe that the market in education would really produce the best schools. Where children are concerned, state paternalism, which is not by definition in all circumstances a vice, does emphatically come into its own.

The second objection lies in the inadequate level of many of the schools which would in practice be the only choices open to most parents. If we really had achieved the 'Austin Seven' standard in schools the situation might well be different. In practice I believe the voucher system would mean that the good schools would get bigger and better, but for many generations of school children the bad schools would not be eliminated. They would simply get relatively, if not absolutely, worse and worse. Professor Peacock talks about a once for all capital payment from the State to improve these schools. They need something far more radical than that. At present we are far too complacent and unambitious about our schools. If the choice really were between some that are good and some that are better, then perhaps the Professor's proposals might be translated into practical policy. As things are, over the next 15 to 20 years we need to put all we can possibly afford into raising the level of our very many below-standard schools.

*Local Charges – Means Tested – To Improve State Schools?*

This does not, I admit, deal with the point that parents would be willing to pay something towards improved education. It is possible that a scheme could be devised which could tap this money, without diverting resources from the poorer quality schools which it is vital to build up. Once a school has reached a really satisfactory standard in terms of both quality and quantity of staff, laboratories, library, playing fields and buildings, no more public money should go directly to that school for additional improvements until those below that level come up to standard, and that is likely to be a long time. If, however, at local level the governing body were able to make additional improvements and to charge parents for them, then these charges could be means tested and, within a defined limit, parents unable to pay could claim back the charge from public funds. For example, a school with a good art department might set out to develop an excellent art department. Parents would know that a very high level of art teaching could be obtained at that school for an additional payment. No pupil able to obtain admission would be barred because of the parents' means, but many parents who could pay would, and money not otherwise available would be fed into education. The same principle might well apply to the provision of boarding as distinct from tuition expenses at state boarding schools, institutions which we certainly need to develop.

## Stronger Case for Opting Out of Health Service

The Health Service is unlike the Education Service in that in the majority of cases the choice is made by the adult for himself, not by a parent for a child. To this extent, a stronger case can be made out for removing the restrictions in choice. But in the Health Service as in the Education Service, the starting point must be a freely available service for all of a really good minimum standard. Where this is assured the opportunity to buy additional benefits, like greater privacy and tastier food, has everything to recommend it.

It is the danger in all such schemes that improvements for those who wish to pay for them are bought at the price of lowering the essential basic standard. This will vary in different situations. In some places space, for example, is in very short supply. In others it is not. Where privacy for some means real overcrowding for others it should not be possible to buy privacy. But where it does not there seems no reason why a person who has economised in entertainments and alcohol in order to buy peace and quiet when ill, should not be permitted to do so.

Of course, such suggestions raise nearly as many problems as they solve, but the aim throughout should be to achieve high basic standards, and to give priority to this, but beyond this point to encourage the maximum of choice for the additional advantages for which people are prepared to pay. It will be objected that I want the best of both worlds. I do. Why not?

# Chapter 13

# Taking Stock

### I: Was It Worth It?

The most colourful character in our family history was Great Grandfather Isaac Turner. He married three times, the first time being at Gretna Green to which the couple had fled from Blaydon, Tyneside — they were quickly forgiven. He remarried on the death of his first wife but his second one also died not much later and he is alleged to have been well looked after in his old age by his third, who was the resident licensee of The Percy Arms in Newcastle-on-Tyne. He was a great betting man as well as a horse dealer, and ran horses at the famous Blaydon Races, but none of these activities helped his purse. He left very little property when he died. Before that sad event, his immediate relations went to see him with the object of persuading to give up, belatedly, a dissolute life. Isaac was asked about his financial affairs and responded by saying that he had just about broken even over his lifetime. There, they argued, you have suffered by your own hand — implying, perhaps, that he risked his salvation. 'Oh no,' he is supposed to have replied, 'think of the fun I had!'

I was often asked by colleagues whether I had not wasted my time by getting involved with the devious ways of politicians and had risked what professional reputation I might claim to have both by this suspect association and the loss of time which could have been otherwise more profitably spent on intellectual improvement. Of course, time is always scarce and these different objectives compete with one another. So they posed a fair question.

In fact, I was beginning to move 'upstream' in the advice 'game', lured there by invitations to serve on government *ad hoc* committees, at home and abroad, set up to make recommendations on particular policy measures, reports for 'think tanks', notably the Anglo-German Foundation, the Institute of Economic Affairs and the Brookings Institution, and eventually I spent three years as full-time Chief Economic Adviser of the Department of Trade and Industry (1973–76). But these activities, to the extent that they were grounded on the earlier experience I have described, leave the question unanswered, calling for an apologia of some sort. Here it is.

### II: The Complementarity of Political Experience

This experience on the fringe of politics complemented to a large degree the important professional requirement of knowing how to study economic motivation. Knowledge of the workings of human institutions is an essential part of the process of constructing the building blocks on which theories of human action were based. 'Institutional economics' still tends to be associated with scholars of economic history who, after detailed study of industrial development, come to the conclusion that economic theories are flawed by the naivety of their behavioural assumptions. However in my early professional life I learnt through association with Ronald Coase and Basil Yamey at LSE that in fact the analytical framework of economic theory was sound enough to act as a powerful tool of empirical analysis of private business behaviour. It also delineated more clearly why business efficiency was positively related to the degree of competition, even in an imperfect form, provided that the customer always had available alternative sources of supply.

Liberal sympathies and their relation to public policies required attention to be concentrated on the economic behaviour of politicians, senior bureaucrats in government departments and agencies and senior executives of nationalised industries, who were largely unaffected by the cold wind of competition. This was not to say that they necessarily operated 'illiberally', but it allowed them a considerable degree of discretion.

Attachment to the fortunes of a political party is a common method nowadays for viewing discretionary behaviour at close quarters. Indeed, adherence to a small party turned out to have advantages denied those of comparable experience and age who acquired their knowledge by membership of larger and more influential centres of political power. As I have indicated, one rose quickly 'through the ranks', because of the paucity of candidates to produce ideas and their translation into liberal economic policies. One learnt quickly that any association with new ideas risked exposure to brutal and relentless criticism in forums of debate, notably the broadsheets, whereas contemporaries working for larger parties were more likely to be employed as research boffins out of the public eye. Their bright ideas would have to go through a filtering process. often resulting in their emasculation, before they would be presented to the world as emanating from their political superiors.[1]

Above all, a small group of activists widely perceived by the public as belonging to a spent, if determined to survive, political force was more likely to reconsider its principles of action. Liberals suffered from the disadvantage that what they had fought for as the champions of political and economic freedom had been incorporated in the agenda of both the Conservative and Labour parties. It was important to establish that there was plenty left for them to do and which could have a separate political appeal. It still surprises me that their leaders, several of them fully familiar with the philosophy of liberalism, were willing to trust their 'greenhorns' with the task of identifying how its principles could

---

[1]   I recall how Lionel Robbins in his youth, similarly anxious to reform the world, worked for a while as assistant to the Labour politician, Arthur Greenwood, working on a proposal to nationalise the drink trade. For the outcome of this experience and Lionel's superb account of his fear that the promised social revolution was an unlikely occurrence, see his *Autobiography of an Economist*, Macmillan, 1971, pp. 71–73.

be reflected in recommendations that could be embodied in a policy statement which had both integrity and political appeal. In retrospect, it seems even more surprising that younger members of the Unservile State Group never openly questioned their own ability to be up to the job.

### III: Modelling Political Motivation

When Jack Wiseman and I had completed our time series of UK government expenditure growth, we might have been content to claim that this was the first time such a study had been undertaken (see Chapter 9 above). However, not content with a useful number-crunching exercise we sought an explanation of the process of growth.

After studying the rather sparse literature on the determinants of long-term government expenditure growth, we came up with a testable hypothesis known as the 'displacement effect' that contains two elements: (i) typically, there is a permanent excess demand for public expenditure reflected in estimated financing requirements that exceed some 'tolerable' level of taxation; and (ii) major social disturbances, such as war and depressions are periods when citizens accept additional tax increases and introduce higher tolerance levels which remain after the event. This became known as the Peacock-Wiseman displacement hypothesis.[2]

---

[2]   The final product, which appeared shortly before our pamphlet on educational vouchers, excited some interest even amongst politicians, Jo Grimond in particular. Academic debate ranged from approval of both the methodology and the conclusions to detailed attempts to refute them by subjecting them to statistical tests. Both Jack and myself were amazed. We had not sought to produce a conclusion of such generality that committed us to what happened in the rest of the world and were careful to point out that our study contained a sample of one country over a limited period of time. Even nearly forty years later, with several joint articles with Jack that did not stem the combined flow of criticism and approval behind one, I felt obliged to point out to the growing army of econometricians who examined our data and sought to refute our conclusions that their own results were flawed. Fortunately an econometrically literate colleague — Professor Alex Scott of Edinburgh Business School, Heriot-Watt University — confirmed that the tests used for examining

This delving into a contemporary academic pursuit was not only a demonstration of the close links between learning about the workings of the political system and ongoing research interests. It also raised important questions about political motivation that we had summarized in the form of its outcome, but had not pursued the matter of its origins. Was there any parallel here between the traditional examination of economic behaviour of individual consumers and producers and that of politicians, particularly those seeking to form governments? Certainly, we knew that the question had been put and answers given by economically literate thinkers from de Tocqueville onwards; and I had edited a book with Richard Musgrave of writings on the subject, published first in 1958 and still in print (see our *Classics in the Theory of Public Finance*, Macmillan, London). Our book and growing involvement in the contemporary political discourse therefore made me well prepared for the rapid development in the study of the economics of government associated with the theory of public choice.

I suppose that, like a large number of economists interested in public policy, I would have been disposed to ignore this development as no more than an irritating attempt to question the disposition of those of who had invested heavily in economic theory as a source of guidance on 'sensible' economic policies. However, this would have been to ignore what I had learnt about the governmental *process* of which political motivation must be a major constituent.

In 1957, Antony Downs had published a book entitled *An Economic Theory of Democracy* in which he developed a model of political motivation which he hoped would increase our understanding of political behaviour in a democratic system. It required him to make some careful assumptions, notably how to devise an acceptable indicator

---

public expenditure growth were not always appropriate and we were able to show that most of the econometric testing was based on an inappropriate definition of government. For example, they commonly left nationalised industries out of its definition. It is gratifying that the 'displacement hypothesis' is included in Segura and Braun's *An Eponymous Dictionary of Economics*, Edward Elgar, 2004, pp. 197–98!

of political behaviour, and to define the political situation to which the model would apply and also, very important, the decision rule which would determine which political party would be elected to govern. Correspondingly, he was bound to consider how political decisions fitted into the basket of objectives of voters, which must include some estimate of the perceived benefits from supporting one particular group of politicians rather than another.

I cannot do justice in short space to the subtlety and depth of analysis of Down's thesis. The essential point that impinges directly on my experiences lies in his extension of the idea of rational choice used in analysis of individual behaviour in market situations to political behaviour. Put in very general terms, politicians only promote particular policies that are a means for obtaining and keeping hold of power. Policies must be formulated so that they win elections. Whether these policies embody the party's principles as embodied in some sacred text such as a Manifesto depends on the voting strength of the 'party faithful'. It is tempting to make a diversion to discuss Down's thesis, and his own development of it and attempts to persuade us of its operational significance, but I desist. The important point is that Downs' book convinced me that my 'diversion' into political debate raised questions about the nature of government that were really only touched upon given its concentration on the legislative process. I had already seen the importance of politics in the execution of policy and therefore in the analysis of bureaucratic behaviour and how it was influenced by the important circumstance of lack of competition and of non-market organisation made necessary by the provision of public services which could not be priced. Adam Smith had pondered over the question as to how to maintain efficiency in government services provision, given his still widely accepted value judgment, namely that the object of their provision was to serve the public.[3]

---

[3]  I was later to write at length on the history of public choice analysis which paid tribute to early writings on the subject. See *Public Choice*

Additionally, I was struck by the importance that the pioneers of this new 'Constitutional Economics', notably James Buchanan and Gordon Tullock, were to place on the devising of constitutional arrangements designed to replicate competitive pricing. Moreover they conveyed the impression that the kernel of a solution to the promotion of 'liberalism' (in the Continental but not the American sense) as a political philosophy lay in 'ideal' constitutional arrangements. This puzzled me, as it may you!

The combination of my political and professional interests prescribed that I had a lot of reading to catch up on! Any doubts about what to do to retain one's interest in political economy, to satisfy my colleagues that I was still intellectually alive and my students that I provided plenty for them to argue about were resolved. There remains the question as to whether, as a result of 're-tooling', which must also include knowing enough mathematics to follow its penetration into public economics, I needed to adjust my views as to what liberalism was all about.

There remained the unanswered question: how did this agenda fit with 'an anxiety to do good', other than to oneself?

### III: An Awkward Answer to a Difficult Question

In 1969, after an exhausting if exhilarating six years combining helping to start off the University of York, losing the battle over liberal social policy within the Party and plunged into boning up again on fiscal policy, I was due a sabbatical. There was a temptation to cross the Pond again to the US—I had been welcomed as a visiting professor at Johns Hopkins University in 1958 and invited to return. Margaret, right as usual in all essential matters, persuaded me otherwise—this would finish up, not as a battery charging operation, but by my becoming a casualty of exhaustion. Providentially, a letter arrived the next day inviting me to spend six months as a research professor at the Univer-

*Analysis in Historical Perspective* (Mattioli Lectures), Cambridge University Press (Paperback Edition), 1997.

sity of Torino seconded to the Einaudi Foundation with its excellent library and offer of secretarial help. I could work on anything I wished to and would have no teaching obligations. This was too good an opportunity to forego, and I needed a break to read the literature which would enable me to complete a joint work on the economic theory of fiscal policy with my York colleague, Keith Shaw.

The Faculty members at Torino seemed determined that some of the time should be on research of their choosing. Margaret and I had to undergo a rigorous training under their guidance in the qualities of Piedmontese wines, coupled with field work. As the professors had differing views on the classification of wines, the field work had to be very extensively conducted. (On one wine-tasting expedition with Franco Reviglio, later Italy's Minister of Finance, Margaret and I were astonished to witness him tasting and then ordering 1000 bottles of Barbaresco at one go.)

Intellectual discourse was not left out, clearly not possible when your host professor was Francesco Forte, also to become Italian Minister of Finance and already internationally known for his contributions to public choice theory. Our discussions has a lasting influence on the attempt to re-discover what sort of liberal I purported to be.

In particular, although we might disagree about the appropriate policies for governments to adopt in given situations, we were at one in making it clear that policy principles had to rest upon a coherent, explicit political philosophy. This view was our reflection, not on the propensity for politicians to have to compromise in their principles in order to obtain election votes, but on the growing tendency in the professional literature in economics of liberalism purely with the decision rules operating in democratic systems of government. It was then I recalled what Hayek had written in his *Constitution of Liberty* (1960) — which I had reviewed a decade before — about the status of majority rule in liberal philosophy: 'Liberalism regards it as desirable that only what the majority accepts should in fact be law, but does not accept that this is necessarily good law. Its aim, indeed, is to persuade the majority to accept certain principles' (p. 103).

In now devoting more attention to what had been happening in the academic study of the economics of public policy, I was to come across a disturbing feature of its application. By regarding political choice not only as the instrument for recording the wishes of an electorate but also as the primary expression of liberalism, one fell into the trap that if majority rule led to 'illiberal' results, then this could justify the making of decisions in the interests of the electorate by dictatorial means. My experience close to the political scene led me to be very wary of any such conclusion, quite apart from one's liberal sympathies that would lead one to question whether the remedy was not worse than the disease. In any case, if I learnt one thing from my experience, it was that to seek perfection in political institutions postulated a search for unanimity, whereas 'true' liberals knew that universal agreement on the translation of principles into practice was a chimera. It would lead nowhere—which is what the term Utopia really means![4]

Enough said about the positive influence of my Liberal experiences on my intellectual interests; but was the 'anxiety to do good' matched by positive results? In the trade jargon, would your performance indicators display movements in the direction of *net* improvements in the welfare of others? A conventional answer would be to direct attention to the judgment of one's own profession, but that is surely illegitimate. I was subsequently lucky in that regard, probably the function of good health and retention of interest in professional as well as political matters. However, retaining

---

[4] This is the merest hint at my later engagement in a long and continuing controversy on the best economic policies, which had to be based on one's views on how economies worked and the appropriateness and effectiveness of which policies should be used. When I returned to look at this question in detail, I benefited enormously from collaboration with my erstwhile colleague at York, Charles Rowley, who fortunately was already completely familiar with the patois of welfare economics and the growing use of mathematical presentation of its basic propositions. This is particularly evident in our book *Welfare Economics: A Liberal Restatement*, Martin Robinson, 1975 (see the Preface).

one's reputation with one's professional colleagues and one's students may be a necessary but hardly a sufficient guide. It would also fail to take into account the costs of one's actions falling on one's family and friends.

I shall stand by a true story about a distinguished American colleague, Paul MacAvoy, who was a member of the US Council of Economic Advisers some years ago. On a visit to Buckingham University, my final full-time academic base, he gave a seminar on his experiences to some Economics students. One of them asked for his view on whether he thought he had done any good by his membership. In a small way, yes, he replied. The best and most striking proof of this, he said, was to win a long and exhausting battle with the US Department of Labour (DoL) over the rights of some cattle drovers who came annually to Montana from Spain to settle in Montana herds for the summer, and noted for their scarce skills in driving to and tending them in the mountain pastures. The DoL claimed that this was contrary to labour legislation and the drovers should no longer be given visas allowing this long-established practice. Paul forcefully argued that they were performing a vital, specialised service that helped the agricultural economy of Montana in a positive way. The DoL tried to involve the Federal environmental authorities with a view to proving that the drovers' habits were insanitary. In the end, Paul won but not quite outright. A condition was laid down that the vehicles transporting the drovers to the mountains had to be equipped with Portaloos!

To some students, this seemed a frivolous answer but would they have been more impressed by some set speech about Paul's membership of an august body putting out prestigious reports on the state of the economy?

So, when asked whether I did any good by giving economic advice, I remember Paul's answer. I served as Chair of the Scottish Arts Council and as a Member of the Arts Council of Great Britain in the 1980s. My only claim to have done any positive good was to lobby — it was like pushing at an open door — the Minister of the Arts, then that much-liked politician Richard Luce, on an equally unusual matter.

Perhaps the poorest paid artistes in the world are the members of the *corps de ballet* of a company on tour. British tax laws lay down that one cannot claim deduction against income tax of expenses incurred in travelling to one's regular place of work. I discovered that the *corps de ballet* of the Scottish Ballet, based in Glasgow, were being threatened with a liability to tax on their travel and accommodation expenses which were to be regarded as part of their exiguous incomes. Anyone who has experience of other tax regimes will know that our tax authorities are regarded as models of integrity and even understanding — and I say this despite my early experiences at the hands of FA Cockfield (see Chapter 6)! I supplied Richard with a memorandum on this attack on the poorly paid. Together we persuaded the Inland Revenue that the ballet's place of work was Glasgow and not a series of touring venues. Self-satisfaction engulfed me on hearing of this 'concession'. 'Meine Pflicht hab' ich getan', I sang from *Fidelio* in my cracked voice. But if I satisfied myself that 'I have done my duty', others would rightly argue that it was the very least I could do.

'A straw in the wind?' — more likely a case of one swallow not making a summer. I cannot in any case think of a suitable clutch of indicators making up some measure of 'doing good', far less some way of trading them off against one another, particularly if one's output is ideas rather than some substantial, measurable entity. This has lead me back to think of my father, the entomologist, and his dedication to the cause of the common soldier in trying to find ways of ridding him of a debilitating disease and which required him to submit himself to the ordeal of infection. I know goodness when I see it. Now I hope that I remain active enough to write about his early struggles when he was much the same age as I was when I sought a career. At least I shall learn more about goodness and maybe others will as well.

# Index of Names

# Index of Subjects